WORds
TO LIVE BY

words
TO LIVE BY

JO PETTY

BRISTOL PARK BOOKS

Published by:

BRISTOL PARK BOOKS, INC

252 W. 38th Street, New York, NY 10018

First Bristol Park Books Paperback edition published in 2014
Bristol Park Books is a registered trademark of Bristol Park Books, Inc.

Library of Congress Control Number: 2012949029
ISBN: 978-0-88486-565-0

Cover and text design by LaBreacht Design
Printed in the United States of America

introduction

THE TIMELESS WORDS of inspiration celebrating the basic
virtues of love, goodness, meekness, patience, hope, joy and
peace are the cornerstone of Jo Petty's inspirational works.

Carefully chosen proverbs, quotations, verses and sayings will
help you discover the keys to practicing and celebrating values
to anchor your life.

Gathered together in this unique collection, *Words to Live By*
will give you a spiritual uplift every time you read and re-read
these eloquent heartfelt sayings.

contents

Love 9

Goodness 47

Meekness 101

Patience 155

Hope 205

Joy 247

Peace 285

about the author 319

Love is the greatest thing in the world!

❀

Jesus loves the little children
All the children of the world—
Red and yellow, black and white,
All are precious in His sight.

❀

Everyone of us is the object of God's care
as thought we were the only one in the world.

❀

God does not play favorites.

❀

No person is outside the scope of God's love.

❀

When God said "whosoever," He included me!

❀

God loved us so much that He send His Son,
Jesus, to earth to show us the way to heaven.

God's love will meet my every need.

❀

I could talk forever
Of Jesus' love divine—
Of all His care and tenderness
For your life and for mine.

❀

God knows us better than we know ourselves, and He loves us better, too.

❀

All loves are but a reflection of God's love for us.

❀

I love God because He first loved me.

❀

If I truly love God, I shall love all others.

❀

To live above with saints we love
O friend, that will be glory.
To live below with saints we know
Is quite a different story.

God loves me in spite of my faults.

❁

I should love others in spite of their faults.

❁

If I love, I love God.

❁

Where love is, there God is.

❁

God is present everywhere and
every person is God's creature.

❁

Hate is like sand in a piece of machinery
and love is like oil.

❁

There is no fear in love; but perfect love casts out fear.

❁

God has not given me the spirit of fear;
but of power, and of love, and of a sound mind.

He who keeps His word,
in him is the love of God perfected.

❁

He that has pity upon the poor lends unto the Lord;
and that which he has given will He pay him again.

❁

God's tender mercies and lovingkindnesses have been ever of old.

❁

I am poor and needy; yet the Lord thinks of me!

❁

The angel of the Lord encamps round about them that fear Him,
and delivers them.

❁

God is a father of the fatherless and a judge of the widows.

❁

In Thee, O Lord, do *I* put my trust:
Cast *me* not off in the time of old age;
forsake *me* not when my strength fails.

Even to your old age I am God;
I have made, and I will bear, I will carry, and deliver you.

❀

Jesus came that *I* might have life
and that *I* might have it more abundantly.

❀

God has commanded me to keep His precepts diligently.

❀

If we have love one to another,
all men will know that we are Jesus' followers.

❀

A friend loves at all times, and a brother is born for adversity.

❀

Greater love has no man that this,
that a man lay down his life for his friend.

❀

If *I* love the world,
the love of the Father is not in *me*.

All that is in the world, the lust of the flesh,
and the lust of the eyes, and the pride of life,
is not of the Father, but is of the world...
but he that does the will of God abides forever.

❁

Love shall cover the multitude of sins.

❁

Love thinks no evil.

❁

Love is not easily provoked.

❁

Love is not selfish.

❁

Love endures all things.

❁

If *I* hear Jesus' sayings and do them, *I* shall be like a wise man,
who built his house upon a rock: and the rain descended, and
the floods came, and the winds blew, and beat upon his house;
and it fell not: for it was founded on a rock.

Love works no ill to his neighbor:
therefore love is the fulfilling of the law.

He that says he is in the light,
and hates his brother is in darkness.

Mercy unto *you*, and peace, and love be multiplied.

Many waters cannot quench love,
neither can floods drown it.

Love is the bond of everything perfect.

If we love one another, God dwells in us,
and His love is perfected in us.

Owe no man any thing, but to love one another:
for he who loves another has fulfilled the law.

If your enemy is hungry,give him bread to eat;
and if he is thirsty, give him water to drink.

❁

If I love only those who love me,
what reward have I?

❁

If I do not forgive men their trespasses,
neither will my Father forgive my trespasses.

❁

Who stops his ears at the cry of the poor,
he also shall cry himself, but shall not be heard.

❁

Increase and abound in love one toward another,
and toward all men.

❁

Love is of God; and everyone that loves is born of God,
and knows God.

❁

God's word is truth.

I shall love the Lord my God with all my heart, and with all my soul,
and with all my mind. This is the first commandment. And
the second is like, namely this, I shall love my neighbor as myself.

If I set my love on God, He will answer me, when I call:
He will be with me in trouble; He will deliver me, and honor me.
With long life will He satisfy me, and show me His salvation.

Cast me not away from Your presence;
and take not Your Holy Spirit from me.
Restore unto me the joy of Your salvation
and uphold me with Your free Spirit.

I am not worthy of Christ if I love son or daughter
or father or mother more than I love Him.

God is love; and he that dwells in love dwells in God,
and God in him.

If I love God, I love my brother also.

Love in deed and in truth rather than in word.

❁

If I have no compassion for my brother in need,
the love of God dwells not in me.

❁

All things whatsoever I would that me should do to me,
I must do even so to them.

❁

I must from my heart forgive my brother his trespasses.

❁

If I love Jesus, I will keep His commandments.

❁

Bless the Lord, O my soul: and all that is within me, bless His holy name.

❁

Heaven and earth shall pass away: but Jesus' words shall not pass away.

❁

Jesus calls me friend; for He has made known to me
all things He heard of His Father.

We are more than conquerors,
through Him that loved us.

Not every one who says Lord, Lord,
shall enter into the kingdom of heaven;
but he that does the will of our Father in heaven.

Wear a breastplate of faith and love;
and for a helmet, the hope of salvation.

Now abides faith, hope, and love,
but the greatest of these is love.

God will never leave me, nor forsake me.

Jesus came to seek and to save those who are lost.

Behold, what manner of love
the Father has bestowed upon me.

The eternal God is my refuge,
and underneath are His everlasting arms.

❁

Neither death, nor life, nor angels, nor principalities, nor powers,
nor things present, nor things to come, nor height, nor depth, nor any
other creature, shall be able to separate me from the love of God.

❁

God has made of one blood all nations of men
for to dwell on all the face of the earth.

❁

He that loves not knows not God; for God is love.

❁

Jesus is the true Light, who lights every man that comes into the world.

❁

The Lord has appeared of old unto me, saying,
Yea, I have loved you with an everlasting love:
therefore with lovingkindness have I drawn you.

❁

Love rejoices in truth.

God so loved the world, that He gave His only
begotten Son, that whosoever believes in Him
should not perish, but have everlasting life.

If God so loved us, we ought also to love one another.

Herein is love, not that I loved God,
but that He loved me.

God sent not His son into the world to condemn the world;
but that the world through Him might be saved.

God forgives all my iniquities; He heals all my diseases;
He redeems my life from destruction;
He crowns me with lovingkindness and tender mercies.

By love serve one another.

Grace be with all them that love our Lord.

All the king's horses and all the king's men cannot make us love,
but God can give us a heart capable of loving.

❋

God's love is in the sunshine's glow,
His life is in the quickening air,
When lightnings flash and storm winds blow,
There is His power; His law is there.

God of the earth, the sky, the sea,
Maker of all things above, below,
Creation lives and moves in Thee,
Your present life through all does flow.

❋

For a small moment God has forsaken me,
but with great mercies will He receive me.
With everlasting kindness will He have mercy on me.

❋

God has no other child like me. I am unique.
I have a beauty all my own.

❋

Obedience to god is the most infallible evidence
of a sincere and supreme love for Him.

Love one another:
for he that loves another has fulfilled the law.

❀

All our loves are fed from the fountain of Infinite Love.

❀

Love is not an art—it is life.

❀

A little girl went into the cathedral during the week when
it was empty. When she came out, she was asked what she did
while in there. She replied, "Oh, I just loved God a little."

❀

Life is an education in His love.

❀

We are successful if we have learned to love.

❀

True love always finds a way to communicate.

❀

If I neglect my love for my neighbor,
in vain do I profess my love for God.

Remember the story of the two bears?
Bear and forbear.

❀

Let brotherly love continue.

❀

Love is happier in the happiness of another
than in its own happiness.

❀

Mutual love is the crown of all our bliss.

❀

Like sunlight through a prism,
love breaks into many parts.

❀

Love suffers long when necessary.

❀

Love is ever kind.

❀

Love does not exalt itself.

Love seeks not its own.

Love never fails.

A friend loves at all times.

And though I have the gift of prophecy, and
understand all mysteries, and all knowledge;
and though I have all faith, so that I could remove
mountains, and have not love, I am nothing.

The Bible teaches that if I confess my sins to God,
He will forgive me just like my mother would kiss
my disobedient acts into everlasting oblivion.

Do not rehash something
God has refused to remember.

Love founded on true virtue never dies.

Love is wisdom.

❀

Lie down on the bosom of God's infinite love.

❀

Love is power.

❀

Smiling is love.

❀

Love gives itself, it is not bought.

❀

Love one human being purely and warmly
and you will love all.

❀

Love is the greatest thing that God can give us,
for He Himself is Love;
and it is the greatest thing we can give to God.
It does the work of all the other graces
without any instrument but its own immediate virtue.

Love is the living essence of the Divine Nature
which beams full of goodness.

If I truly love, I have God in me, for God is Love.

True love is eternal, infinite, and always like itself.

Love forgives.

Do not complicate what Jesus
has made clear enough for a child
to comprehend about forgiveness.
To be forgiven by God,
we must forgive all who offend us.

Forgiveness is release.

Forgiveness is reconciliation.

Forgiveness is a new beginning.

❁

For if you forgive men their trespasses,
your heavenly Father will also forgive you.

❁

The education of the soul for eternity should begin
and be carried on at the fireside.

❁

Life is but one continual course of instruction—
we can learn something from every person we meet.
Our parents are our first church and school.
Parents write on the heart of the child the first faint characters
which time deepens into strength so that nothing can efface them.

❁

Let love be without dissimulation.
Abhor that which is evil; cleave to that which is good.

❁

I still sing one of the very first songs I learned as a child:
Jesus loves me! This I know
For the Bible tells me so.

Having learned that Jesus loves me,
I consider this the greatest lesson anyone can learn.

❁

O yes, it is better to have a house without a roof
than a family unsheltered by God's love.

❁

God has ordered that, being in need of each other,
we should learn to love each other
and bear one another's burdens.

❁

The cure for all the ills and wrongs,
the sorrows and the crimes of humanity
all lie in the one word, "LOVE."
Each and every one of us has the power
of working miracles if we truly love.

❁

When I speak of love, I mean the love
which loves because of its own inherent nature,
not because of the existence or worth of its object
—spontaneous, automatic love.

Could we judge all deeds by motives,
See the good and bad within,
Surely we would love the sinner,
All the while we loathe the sin.

❁

God has taught us all truth in teaching us to love.

❁

A person who always loves never seems to grown old
since so many charms are preserved.

❁

Home is where love is best taught and learned.

❁

To be a Christian does not mean that I have arrived,
but that I am on my way!

❁

If the tender, profound, and sympathizing love
practiced and recommended by Jesus were paramount
in every heart, the loftiest and most glorious idea
of human society would be realized.

I am the only me, and God loves me!

Jesus, what did You find in me
That You have dealt so lovingly?
How great the joy that You have brought
O far exceeding hope or thought.

The end of all learning is to know God, and
out of that knowledge to love and imitate Him.

If our love were but more simple,
We should take Him at His Word,
And our lives would be all sunshine
In the sweetness of the Lord.

What shall I do to love? Believe.
What shall I do to believe? Love.

No door is too difficult for the key of love to open.

We love ourselves notwithstanding our faults,
and we ought to love our neighbor in a like manner.

❁

We may give without loving,
but we cannot love without giving.

❁

The love of God is broader
Than the measure of man's mind;
And the heart of the Eternal
Is most wonderfully kind.

❁

The way I want my friend to treat me
is exactly how I should treat my friend.

❁

The language of love is understood by all.

❁

All good gifts around us
Are sent from heaven above;
Then thank the Lord, O thank the Lord
For all His love.

The heart has reasons that reason does not understand.

❁

Help me to do the things I should
To be to others kind and good,
In all I do in work or play—
To grow more loving every day.

❁

Love tells a friend when he gets on the wrong road.

❁

Love is the law of life.

❁

Do unto others as though you were the others.

❁

Jesus is my best friend!

❁

Love and you shall be loved.

❁

If nobody loves me, it is my own fault.

The greatest joy is to love and be loved.

❀

He prays best who loves best.

❀

God, Whose Name is Love, will send the best.

❀

We would love each other better if we only understood.

❀

We learn to love better as we grow older.

❀

Love is enough.

❀

Life is nothing but a growing in love.

❀

The only way to have a friend is to be one.

❀

A friend is a present you give yourself.

A cheerful friend is like a sunny day.

A true friend is forever a friend.

A friend can seem as close to you as your brother,
sometimes closer.

A friend knows all about you—even the bad part
—and still loves you.

A friend is one with whom you may dare to be yourself.

You can act any old way with your friend,
buy you really shouldn't.

Even when I make a fool of myself, my friend still loves me.

Love is patient.

Love is willing to wait.

❁

Love grows.

❁

Love sees what the eye cannot.

❁

Love hears what the ear cannot.

❁

Love doesn't get tired.

❁

Love outlasts everything else.

❁

The worst kind of heart trouble
is not to have love in your heart.

❁

Do I love things and use people
or love people and use things?

The most I can do for any person is to love him.

All loves should be stepping-stones
to the love of God.

Work is love you can see.

I must love you like I love myself.

Sometimes it's your turn and sometimes it's my turn.

Love reminds a friend when he makes a mistake
if he does not seem to know.

Love your enemies, do good to them that hate you…
that you may be children of your Father which is in heaven:
for He makes His sun to shine on the evil and on the good,
and sends rain on the just and unjust.

Love can't be wasted.

❀

Love never fails!

❀

Hatred is like an acid.
It can do more damage to the vessel in which it is stored
than to the object on which it is poured.

❀

Not where I breathe, but where I love, I live.

❀

Religion is love in action.

❀

Love is the root of all virtues.

❀

Love behaves.

❀

The test of our love for God
is the love we have one for another.

If I love Jesus, I will do what He says.

Heaven and earth shall some day pass away,
but not Jesus' words.

If I love you, I will not lie to you nor about you.

If I love my parents, I will honor them
and do nothing to make them unhappy.

If I love the poor, I will give to them.

I must even love my enemies.

I must love one who says something bad about me.

If I remember to do Jesus' words, I shall know the truth
and the truth will make me free.

Love is one language everybody understands.

❀

Love doesn't think bad things.

❀

Love does not get angry easily.

❀

Love doesn't brag about me.

❀

Love God and all things will work together for good.

❀

We love when it makes us happpier for the other person
to be happy than to be happy ourselves.

❀

Love loves to help one another.

❀

He who does not love does not know God
for God is love.

We owe our love to every person because God
made every person and God loves every person.

❀

If I love, that takes care of everything.

❀

Now if I love like this, I know God's love is in me,
for my love would not be that loving.

❀

If I love, then I know God lives inside me.

❀

Love praises others.

❀

Love puts up with an awful lot.

❀

Love is funny—the more you give away
the more you seem to have left.

❀

A man who has many friends must show himself friendly.

Forget not to entertain strangers:
for thereby some have entertained angels unawares.

❁

Support the weak and cheer the fainthearted.

❁

I should therefore be merciful as my Father also is merciful.

❁

Be followers of God, as dear children; and walk in love.

❁

To whom little is forgiven, the same loves little.

❁

The price of a virtuous woman is far above rubies.
The heart of her husband safely trusts in her.
She will do him good and not evil all the days of her life.
Strength and honor are her clothing; and she shall rejoice in time
to come. She opens her mouth with wisdom; and in her tongue
is the law of kindness. She eats not the bread of idleness.
Her children arise up, and call her blessed; her husband also,
and he praises her. Many daughters have done virtuously,
but she excels them all.

Children should obey their parents
for this is well pleasing unto the Lord.

Foolishness is bound in the heart of a child;
but the rod of correction shall drive it far from him.

In heaven the angels of the little ones do always
behold the face of our Father in heaven.

It is not the will of our Father in heaven
that one of these little ones should perish.

In order that it may be well with me and that I might live long on the
earth, I must honor my father and mother.

He that loves silver shall not be satisfied with silver;
nor he that loves abundance with increase.

The end of the commandment is love out of a pure heart,
and of a good conscience, and of faith unfeigned.

We that are strong ought to bear the infirmities
of the weak, and not to please ourselves.

❀

I must not put a stumbling block or
an occasion to fall in my brother's way.

❀

Weep with them that weep and rejoice with them that do rejoice.

❀

Remember the poor.

❀

If I forgive, I shall be forgiven.

❀

If I judge not and condemn not, I shall not be judged nor condemned.

❀

The unbelieving husband is sanctified by the wife,
and the unbelieving wife is sanctified by the husband...

❀

Life without love would be like the earth without the sun.

goodness

To every one there opens a high way and a low—
And each person decides the way his soul shall go!

❁

No one has a right to do as he pleases,
except when he pleases to do right.

❁

If you do what you should not, you must bear what you would not.

❁

Whatever I sow, that I shall reap.

❁

All things whatsoever I would that others should do to me,
I must do even so to them.

❁

The EYES of the Lord are in every place
beholding the evil and the good.

❁

Even a child is known by his doings,
whether his work be pure, and whether it be right.

Do I practice the behavior I expect from others?

❀

Sow an act and you reap a habit.
Sow a habit and you reap a character.
Sow a character and you reap a destiny.

❀

If you want to put the world right, start with yourself.

❀

He who reforms himself
has done much toward reforming others.

❀

If the whole world followed you,
Followed to the letter,
Tell me—if it followed you,
Would the world be better?

❀

Let us seek not to be better than our neighbors,
but better than ourselves.

❀

Life is not the wick or the candle—it is the burning.

Jesus, Friend of little children,
Be a friend to me;
Take my hand and ever keep me
Close to Thee.
Teach me how to grow in goodness
Daily as I grow;
You have been a child,
And surely You must know.

❖

A man is rich according to what he is,
not according to what he has.

❖

Be what you wish others to become.

❖

Resolve to be better for the echo of it.

❖

If anyone speaks evil of you,
so live that none will believe it.

❖

Reputation is what people think we are.
Character is what God knows we are.

The only way to settle a disagreement
is on the basis of what's right—not who's right.

❁

There is no right way to do the wrong thing.

❁

We've got to build a better man before we build a better world.

❁

One sinner destroys much good.

❁

If you are not able to make yourself what you wish,
how can you expect to mold another to your will?

❁

If I were faultless I would not be so much annoyed
by the defects of others.

❁

The Devil has many tools, but a lie is the handle that fits them all.

❁

You are not better for being praised
nor worse for being blamed.

Doing right is no guarantee against misfortune.

❀

Always tell the truth and you won't need a good memory.

❀

Spend so much time on the improvement of yourself
that you have no time to criticize others.

❀

Do right and leave the results with God.

❀

Liberty is not the right to do as we please,
but the opportunity to do what is right.

❀

The earth is full of the goodness of the Lord.

❀

God is faithful.
While the earth remains, seedtime and harvest, cold and heat,
and summer and winter, and day and night shall not cease.

❀

God is good and he loves us always and in all ways.

All things bright and beautiful,
All creatures great and small;
All things wise and wonderful,
The Lord God made them all.

Each little flower that opens,
Each little bird that sings,
He made their glowing colors,
He made their tiny wings.

He gave us eyes to see them,
And lips that we might tell
How good is God our Father,
Who does all things well.

❀

Be quiet and think on God's goodness.

❀

Cast out the beam from your own eye; and you shall see clearly
to cast the mote out of your brother's eye.

❀

Create in me a clean heart, O.God;
and renew a right spirit within me, I pray.

Let us bear one another's burdens,
and so fulfil the law of Christ.

❀

Feed the hungry, give drink to the thirsty,
take into your home the strangers, clothe the naked,
visit the sick and those in prison.
Inasmuch as we do these things unto the least
of our brothers, we do them unto Jesus.

❀

Speak not evil one of another.

❀

Ever follow that which is good to all men.

❀

Render not evil for evil unto any person.

❀

Be a doer of the word, and not a hearer only,
deceiving your own self.

❀

Don't mistake potatoes for principles or peas for piety.

You are not what you think you are,
but you are what you think.

❁

We see things not as they are, but as we are.

❁

The greatest of faults is to be conscious of none.

❁

Sin is the transgression of the law.

❁

Fools make a mock at sin.

❁

My sins have withheld good things from me.

❁

He who covers his sins shall not prosper:
but whoso confesses and forsakes them shall have mercy.

❁

We don't break God's laws—
we break ourselves on them.

Are you trying to make something for yourself
or something of yourself?

❁

A lie has no legs. It requires other lies to support it.
Tell one lie and you are forced to tell others to back it up.

❁

Conscience is the still small voice
that makes you feel still smaller.

❁

Abstain from all appearance of evil.

❁

Honest gain is the only permanent gain.

❁

For when the One great Scorer comes,
To write against your name,
He writes not that you lost or won
But how you played the game.

❁

To be good is fine, but to be proud of it
ruins the whole thing.

A criminal is nothing else but you and me
at our weakest, found out.

❁

Discover what is true and practice what is good.

❁

Many faults in our neighbor should be of less concern to us
than one of the smallest in ourselves.

❁

Would you like to see the most dangerous animal in the world—
the one that can harm you the most? Look in the mirror.

❁

The hand that's dirty with honest labor
is fit to shake with any neighbor.

❁

As we have opportunity, let us do good unto all men.

❁

No one can be good to others without being good to himself.

❁

To him that knows to do good, and does it not, to him it is a sin.

I am asking when I pray 'O Father' to live here as it is done there.

❁

Pretty is as pretty does.

❁

It shall be well with the righteous: for they shall
eat the fruit of their doing. It shall be ill to the wicked:
for the reward of his hands shall be given to him.

❁

If I am faithful in that which is least,
I shall be faithful also in much.

❁

If I am unjust in the least, I shall be unjust also in much.

❁

To whom much is given, of him much shall be required.

❁

Prove all things; hold fast that which is good.

❁

Lying lips are abomination to the Lord;
but they that deal truly are His delight.

Be holy in all manner of conversation.

❀

The pure in heart shall see God.

❀

If I say I abide in Jesus, I should walk as He walked.

❀

If you talk the talk, baby, walk the walk.

❀

I shall to my own self be true.
If I am true to those around me, I shall be true to myself.

❀

The man who trims himself to suit everybody
will soon whittle himself away.

❀

What you dislike in another, take care to correct in yourself.

❀

Only the best behavior is good enough
for daily use in the home.

Do the best things in the worst times.

❁

Nobody's perfect, but I'm close.

❁

Can my creed be recognized in my deed?

❁

Man looks on the outward appearance;
but God looks on the heart.

❁

Sin is not in things, but in the wrong use of things.

❁

Be what you say and say what you are.

❁

Honesty is always the best policy.

❁

A problem honestly stated is half solved.

❁

Truth cannot be killed with the sword or gun nor abolished by law.

It is easy to tell a lie; but hard to tell only one lie.

❁

It is better to suffer for speaking the truth
than that the truth should suffer for want of speaking it.

❁

Prefer loss before unjust gain.

❁

Oh, what a tangled web we weave,
when first we practice to deceive.

❁

If I am not liberal with what I have, I deceive myself
if I think I would be more liberal if I had more.

❁

If I wish to secure the good of others,
I have already secured my own.

❁

Keep your nose clean so you can smell a phoney.

❁

If the cake is bad, what good is the icing.

From the errors of others a wise man corrects his own.

❁

The prodigal robs his heir; the miser robs himself.

❁

Talent may develop in solitude,
but character is developed in society.

❁

The man who lives by himself and for himself
is apt to be corrupted by the company he keeps.

❁

Progress is not changing, but changing for the better.

❁

Your luck is how treat people.

❁

I am the temple of God and the Spirit of God dwells in me.
I must not defile the temple.

❁

The Spirit Itself bears witness with my spirit,
that I am a child of God.

He who lives to live forever never fears dying.

❁

Live virtuously and you cannot die too soon
nor live too long.

❁

Life is a journey, not a home.

❁

What I am to be, I am now becoming.

❁

The great acts of love are done by those
who are habitually performing small acts of kindness.

❁

Pleasant words are as an honeycomb, sweet to the soul,
and health to the bones.

❁

Nothing multiplies so much as kindness.

❁

Kind feelings make noble the smallest act.

The luxury of doing kindnesses
surpasses every other personal enjoyment.

❋

Kindness is taught by precept and example.

❋

Kindness will convert more sinners than will zeal,
eloquence or learning.

❋

If your enemy is hungry, give him bread to eat;
and if he is thirsty, give him water to drink.

❋

Give kind looks. Do kind acts and
don't forget the warm handshakes.

❋

Politeness comes from within, from the heart.

❋

Politeness is benevolence in small things.

❋

Politeness of the heart is akin to love.

Politeness says, "I would make you happy."

❀

Follow after righteousness, godliness, faith,
love, patience, meekness.

❀

Courtesies of a small nature strike deep to the grateful heart.

❀

It is kindness in a person, not beauty, which wins our love.

❀

Pray for a short memory of all unkindness.

❀

Don't speak of others' faults until you have none of your own.

❀

The words of a wise man's mouth are gracious.

❀

Be courteous to everyone.

❀

Charity suffers long, and is kind.

A pleasant smile accomplishes wonders.

❁

A man that has friends must show himself friendly.

❁

The desire of a man is his kindness.

❁

Do today's duty today.

❁

No person can really be strong, gentle, pure and good,
without the world being better for it, without somebody being helped
and comforted by the very existence of his or her kindness.

❁

Let every one of us please his neighbor
for his good to edification.

❁

My vocation is the simple round of duties
which the passing hour brings.

❁

The post of honor is the path of duty.

Duty by habit turns into pleasure.

❁

It is my duty to be kind to all who cross my path.

❁

There is noble forgetfulness—
that which does not remember injuries.

❁

The bigger the heart, the less room
for the memory of a wrong.

❁

Labor is rest from the sorrows that greets us;
from all the petty vexations that meet us.

❁

Not with the sword's loud clashing
Nor roll of stirring drums,
With deeds of love and mercy
The heavenly kingdom comes.

❁

Be kindly affectioned one to another with brotherly love;
in honor preferring one another.

It is hard for the face to conceal the thoughts of the heart.

Learn the art of mixing gentleness with firmness.
It is better to have headaches for rebuking
when necessary than to have heartaches later.

A word or even a nod from one who loves us carries a lot of weight.

O, for homes ruled according to God's Word!

Our chief wisdom consists in knowing our follies and faults,
so that we may correct them.

I take great comfort in the statement that nobody is perfect
and that I am the perfect example.

Be kind to yourself!

Share your joy if you wish to have more.

How lovely are the faces of
Those who talk with God…
Lit with an inner sureness of
The path their feet have trod;
How gentle is the manner of
Those who walk with Him!

❁

He that does good is of God.

❁

Teach me Thy patience; still with Thee
In closer, dearer company,
In work that keeps faith sweet and strong,
In trust that triumphs over wrong.

❁

Let us not be weary in well doing:
for in due season we shall reap.

❁

I can be kind in looks, words and acts.

❁

Blessed be the Lord: for he has shown me
his marvellous kindness.

Combat another's anger
with a smile and a kind word.

❁

If I take a good look at myself,
I will learn to look at others differently.

❁

Above all, put on charity,
which is the bond of perfectness.

❁

When I have failed to be the kind person I should be, I pray
that my failure may cause someone to want to behave differently.
Sometimes I think I may have learned more
tolerance from the intolerant than the tolerant.
I ask God to take all my failures and somehow, somewhere,
sometime, make them show forth His praise.

❁

Kindness to children and a willingness to conform to the ideal
character of childhood are the marks of a true Christian.

❁

For the mountains shall depart, and the hills be removed;
but my kindness shall not depart from you.

O fill me with Thy fullness, Lord,
Until my very heart overflows,
In kindling thought and glowing word,
Thy love to tell, thy praise to show.

❀

A merry heart does good like a medicine.

❀

The true ornament of any person is virtue,
not clothes or jewels.

❀

Goodness heightens beauty.

❀

Much knowledge will not benefit me if I am not honest.

❀

Jesus is the foundation of my hopes, the object of my faith,
and the subject of my love. He is the model for my conduct.

❀

When my son asked,
"What do you want me to be when I grow up?"
I replied, "A good man."

Even the best of people make mistakes.
But we can learn good through evil and progress to
goodness and greatness through great mistakes.
If my family were perfect, I could not endure the contrast.
My weaknesses help me to understand the weaknesses of others.

❁

Who can understand his errors?
cleanse me from secret faults.

❁

Everything needed to make a saint is in the home.

❁

I shall endeavor not to look back
unless it is to derive useful lessons from past errors and
for the purpose of profiting by dearly bought experience.

❁

A good person is influenced by God Himself.

❁

I am blessed if I have a tender conscience.
I can discern what is evil and avoid it.
If I do not let my conscience become hardened, I can shun evil
as quickly as the eyelid closes itself against a speck of dust.

My conscience is a safe guide
if I keep myself enlightened by the Word of God.

❁

Genuine goodness has love for its essence, humility
for its clothing, the good of others as its employment,
and the honor of God as its end.

❁

Conscience is the voice of the soul.

❁

There will be a golden age only when golden hearts are beating in it.
The religion of Christ reaches and changes the heart,
which no other religion does.

❁

The head truly enlightened will presently have
a wonderful influence in purifying the heart.

❁

I have no right to do as I please unless I please to do right.

❁

The only solution to human problems
is a change in the hearts of people.

Do unto others as though you were the others.

❁

May I always possess firmness and virtue enough to maintain
what is the most enviable of all titles—an honest person.

❁

Deserve honor by your own virtue.

❁

Be like Jesus—this my song,
In the home and in the throng,
Be like Jesus all day long:
I would be like Jesus!

❁

No better heritage can a father bequeath to his children
than a good name.

❁

Instead of spending so much time looking for wealth
to leave to our children, why don't we secure for them
virtuous habits which are worth more than money?

❁

The best way to preserve democracy is to deserve it.

True liberty can never interfere
with the duties and rights of others
who are doing what they ought.

❀

Honor is like the eye, which cannot suffer the least impurity
without damage. It is a precious stone,
the price of which is lessened by a single flaw.

❀

My part is to improve the present moment.

❀

It takes the whole of life to learn how to live.

❀

Ever follow that which is good to all men.

❀

Blessings are upon the head of the just.

❀

Every virtue we possess;
And every victory won;
And every thought of holiness,
Are God's alone.

BEGIN THE DAY WITH GOD
Kneel down to Him in prayer;
Lift up my hear to His abode,
And seek His love to share.

OPEN THE BOOK OF GOD
And read a portion there;
That it may hallow all my thoughts,
And sweeten all my care.

GO THROUGH THE DAY WITH GOD
Whatever my work may be;
Wherever I am—at home, abroad,
He still is near to me.

CONVERSE IN MIND WITH GOD
My spirit heavenward raise;
Acknowledge every good bestowed,
And offer grateful praise.

LIE DOWN AT NIGHT WITH GOD
Who gives His servants sleep;
And when I tread the vale of death
He will guard me and keep me.

Help your brother's boat across,
and lo! your own has reached the shore.

❁

Is there anything in the world more spacious
than the room we have for improvement?

❁

Breathe on me, Breath of God,
Fill me with life anew,
That I may love what though does love,
And do what thou would do.

❁

The eyes of the Lord are in every place
beholding the evil and the good.

❁

God's faithfulness is to all generations.

❁

While the earth remains, seedtime and harvest,
and cold and heat, and summer and winter,
and day and night shall not cease.

He that diligently seeks good procures favor.

God will render glory, honor and peace,
to every man that does good work.

God is no respecter of persons:
but in every nation he that fears God and
works righteousness is accepted with Him.

This *I* recall to *my* mind, therefore *I* have hope.
It is of the Lord's mercies that we are not consumed,
because His compassions fail not.

Not he who commends himself is approved,
but whom the Lord commends.

Cast away from me all *my* transgressions;
and make *me* a new heart and a new spirit.

Learn to do well; seek judgment, relieve the oppressed,
judge the fatherless, plead for the widow.

He has shown *you*, O man, what is good;
and what the Lord requires of *you*:
that *you* do justly, and love mercy,
and walk humbly with *your* God.

Come now, and let us reason together;
says the Lord: though *my* sins be as scarlet,
they shall be white as snow;
though they be red like crimson, they shall be as wool.

Seven things are an abomination to the Lord:
A proud look,
A lying tongue,
Hands that shed innocent blood,
A heart that devises wicked imaginations,
Feet that be swift in running to mischief,
A false witness that speak lies,
And he that sows discord among brethren.

God's word have *I* hid in *my* heart that *I* might not sin against Him.

❁

Withhold not good from them to whom it is due,
when it is in the power of *your* hand to do it.

❁

Though hand join in hand,
the wicked shall not be unpunished;
but the seed of the righteous shall be delivered.

❁

Godliness is profitable unto all things, having promise
of the life that now is, and of that which is to come.

❁

Remove not the ancient landmark, which *your* fathers have set.

❁

The righteous is delivered out of trouble.

❁

Riches profit not in the day of wrath:
but righteousness delivers from death.

A false balance is abomination to the Lord:
but a just weight is His delight.

❀

The fear of the Lord prolongs days:
but the years of the wicked shall be shortened.

❀

The hope of the righteous shall be gladness.

❀

He who walks uprightly walks surely.

❀

The labor of the righteous tends to life; the fruit of the wicked to sin.

❀

In the way of righteousness is life;
and in the pathway thereof there is no death.

❀

Lying lips are abomination to the Lord:
but they that deal truly are His delight.

❀

Jesus came to call sinners to repentance.

The steps of a good man are ordered by the Lord:
and the Lord delights in his way.

❀

He who gets riches and not by right,
shall leave them in the midst of his days,
and at his end shall be a fool.

❀

Honor your father and your mother:
that your days may be long upon the land
which the Lord your God gives you.

❀

Evil pursues sinners:
but to the righteous good shall be repayed.

❀

Let the wicked forsake his way and the unrighteous man
his thoughts: and let him return unto the Lord,
and He will have mercy upon him;
and to our God, for He will abundantly pardon.

❀

A good man obtains favor of the Lord:
but a man of wicked devices will he condemn.

The Lord will not suffer the soul of the righteous to famish:
but He casts away the substance of the wicked.

❁

Let *your* love be sincere.
Abhor that which is evil; cleave to that which is good.

❁

He who hastens to be rich has an evil eye,
and considers not that poverty shall come upon him.

❁

The just man falls seven times, and rises up again:
but the wicked shall fall into mischief.

❁

The candle of the wicked shall be put out.

❁

You shall not respect persons in judgment;
but *you* shall hear the small as well as the great;
... for the judgment is God's.

❁

The just man walks in his integrity;
his children are blessed after him.

Even a child is known by his doings,
whether his work be pure, and whether it be right.

✿

Every way of man is right in his own eyes;
but the Lord ponders the hearts.

✿

He also that is slothful in his work
is brother to him that is a great waster.

✿

The Lord is far from the wicked:
but He hears the prayer of the righteous.

✿

The hoary head is a crown of glory,
if it be found in the way of righteousness.

✿

A whisperer separates chief friends.

✿

He who walks with wise men shall be wise:
but a companion of fools shall be destroyed.

A good man leaves an inheritance to his children's children:
and the wealth of the sinner is laid up for the just.

❧

Go from the presence of a foolish man,
when *you* perceive not in him the lips of knowledge.

❧

He that despises his neighbor sins:
but he that has mercy on the poor, happy is he.

❧

In Christ *I* have redemption through His blood,
even the forgiveness of sins.

❧

He who covers his sins shall not prosper:
but whoso confesses and forsakes them shall have mercy.

❧

The earth is full of the goodness of the Lord.

❧

The righteous cry, and the Lord hears,
and delivers them out of all their troubles.

Oh how great is God's goodness, which He has laid up
for them that fear Him; which He has wrought for them
that trust in Him before the sons of men.

❁

The face of the Lord is against them that do evil.

❁

The eyes of the Lord are upon the righteous,
and His ears are open until their cry.

❁

Remember not the sins of *my* youth,
nor *my* transgressions: according to your mercy
remember *me* for goodness' sake, O Lord.

❁

Order *my* conversation aright and *I* shall see the salvation of God.

❁

He who makes haste to be rich shall not be innocent.

❁

To show favoritism among persons is not good:
because for a piece of bread that man will transgress.

The law of the Lord is perfect, converting the soul:
the testimony of the Lord is sure, making wise the simple.

❖

The eyes of the Lord are over the righteous,
and His ears are open unto their prayers:
but the face of the Lord is against them that do evil.

❖

God's way is perfect.

❖

Every good tree brings forth good fruit;
but a corrupt tree brings forth evil fruit.

❖

Let not presumptuous sins have dominion over *me*.

❖

Cleanse *me*, O God, from secret faults.

❖

Better is a little with righteousness
than great revenues without right.

By the fear of the Lord men depart from evil.

❀

Let *me* search and try *my* ways, and turn again to the Lord.

❀

Lay aside all malice, and all guile, and hypocrisies,
and envies, and all evil speakings.

❀

If *I* know to do good, and do it not, *I* have sinned.

❀

If *my* eye is good, *my* whole body shall be full of light.
If *my* eye be evil, *my* whole body shall be full of darkness.

❀

The path of the just is as the shining light,
that shines more and more unto the perfect day.

❀

Out of the same mouth proceeds blessing and cursing.
With *my* tongue I bless God and I curse men, who are made
after the similitude of God. These things out not to be.

Speak not evil one of another.

By *my* words *I* shall be justified,
and by *my* words *I* shall be condemned.

Feed the hungry, give drink to the thirsty,
take into *your* home the strangers, clothe the naked,
visit the sick and those in prison. Inasmuch as *we* do this
unto the least of *our* brothers, *we* do it unto Jesus.

O praise the Lord… all you people.
For His merciful kindness is great toward us:
and the truth of the Lord endures for ever.

Prove all things; hold fast that which is good.

Ever follow that which is good to all men.

Render not evil for evil unto any man.

Not by works of righteousness which I have done,
but according to His mercy He saved *me*.

❀

The Lord is good unto them that wait for Him,
the soul that seeks Him.

❀

Pure religion and undefiled before God is this,
to visit the fatherless and widows in their affliction,
and to keep *myself* unspotted from the world.

❀

Be a doer of the word, and not a hearer only, deceiving *yourself*.

❀

Be swift to hear, slow to speak, slow to wrath:
for the wrath of man works not the righteousness of God.

❀

I am tempted when *I* am drawn away by *my* own lust, and enticed.

❀

Hear *me*, O Lord; for your lovingkindness is good:
turn unto *me* according to the multitude of your tender mercies.

Out of the abundance of the heart the mouth speaks.

❀

Render therefore unto Caesar the things which are Caesar's;
and unto God the things that are God's.

❀

Take heed not to let any root of bitterness spring up
and trouble *you*, and thereby many be defiled.

❀

Let not mercy and truth forsake *you:*
bind them about *your* neck; write them on the table of *your* heart.

❀

I cannot serve two masters.

❀

The son shall not bear the iniquity of the father,
neither shall the father bear the iniquity of the son:
the righteousness of the righteous shall be upon him,
and the wickedness of the wicked shall be upon him.

❀

If a man be just, and do that which is lawful and right…,
he shall surely live.

All souls are God's:… the soul that sins, it shall die.

❁

The Lord will bless the righteous;
with favor will He compass him as with a shield.

❁

Good and upright is the Lord:
therefore will He teach sinners in the way.

❁

The Lord is good and ready to forgive;
and plenteous in mercy unto all them who call upon Him.

❁

Offer the sacrifices of righteousness,
and put *your* trust in the Lord.

❁

He that walks uprightly, and works righteousness, and speaks
the truth in his heart; he that backbites not with his tongue, nor does
evil to his neighbor, nor takes up a reproach against his neighbor;
in whose eyes a vile person is scorned; but he who honors them
that fear the Lord, who swears to his own hurt, and changes not,
who puts not out his money to usury nor takes a reward against
the innocent; he that does these things shall never be moved.

What God has cleansed, call not common.

❀

The word of God's grace is able to build *me* up, and
to give *me* an inheritance among all them who are sanctified.

❀

Mercy and truth are met together;
righteousness and peace have kissed each other.

❀

We ought to obey God rather than men.

❀

Speak not evil of the ruler of *your* people.

❀

The godly walk not in the counsel of the ungodly, do not stand
in the way of sinners, do not sit in the seat of the scornful,
but delight in the law of the Lord and meditate therein day and night.
The godly shall be like a tree planted by the rivers of the water,
that brings forth his fruit in his season; his leaf shall not wither;
and whatsoever he does shall prosper.

❀

My defense is of God, Who saves the upright in heart.

The ungodly are like the chaff which the wind drives away...
The Lord knows the way of the righteous,
but the way of the ungodly shall perish.

❁

The righteous Lord loves righteousness;
His countenance does behold the upright.

❁

For Your Name's sake, O Lord,
pardon *my* iniquity; for it is great.

❁

Study to show *yourself* approved unto God,
a workman who needs not be ashamed,
rightly dividing the word of truth.
But shun profane and vain babblings:
for they will increase to more ungodliness.

❁

It shall be well with the righteous:
for they shall eat the fruit of their doing.

❁

It is lawful to do well on the sabbath days.

It shall be ill to the wicked:
for the reward of his hands shall be given him.

❀

Woe unto them that call evil good, and good evil;
that put darkness for light, and light for darkness;
that put bitter for sweet, and sweet for bitter!

❀

Let *your* light so shine before men, that they may see
your good works, and glorify *your* Father in heaven.

❀

Provide things honest in the sight of all men.

❀

Blessed are they which do hunger and thirst after righteousness:
for they shall be filled.

❀

You are the salt of the earth… the light of the world.

❀

Judge not according to the appearance,
but judge righteous judgment.

As *I* have opportunity, *I* should do good to all men,
especially unto them who are of the household of faith.

❖

The Lord blots out *my* transgressions for His own sake,
and will not remember *my* sins.

❖

Because sentence against an evil work is not executed speedily,
therefore in the heart of the sons of men
is fully set in them to do evil...
It shall be well with them that fear God,...
but it shall not be well with the wicked.

❖

The Lord is good; His mercy is everlasting;
and His truth endures to all generations.

❖

Whatsoever *I* sow, *I* shall also reap.

❖

A good man shows favor and lends:
he will guide his affairs with discretion.
He shall not be afraid of evil tidings: his heart is fixed,
trusting in the Lord. He has given to the poor.

God will bless them that fear the Lord,
both small and great.

❋

God has not dealt with *me* after *my* sins;
nor rewarded *me* according to *my* iniquities.

❋

As the heaven is high above the earth,
so great is His mercy toward them that fear Him.

❋

God visits the earth, and waters it.

❋

My sins have withholden good things from *me*.

❋

The mercy of the Lord is from everlasting to everlasting
upon them that fear Him, and His righteousness
unto children's children; to such as keep His covenant,
and to those who remember His commandments to do them.

❋

There is not a just man on earth,
that does good, and sins not.

Sin is the transgression of the law.

❁

If *I* confess *my* sins,
God is faithful and just to forgive *me my* sins,
and to cleanse *me* from all unrighteousness.

❁

Who rewards evil for good,
then evil shall not depart from his house.

❁

God causes the grass to grow for the cattle, and herb for
the service of man: that he may bring forth food out of the earth;
and wine that makes glad the heart of man, and oil to make
his face to shine, and bread which strengthens man's heart.

❁

The fear of the Lord is the beginning of wisdom:
a good understanding have all they that do His commandments.

❁

Blessed is the man that fears the Lord, that delights greatly
in His commandments. His seed shall be mighty upon
the earth: the generation of the upright shall be blessed.
Wealth and riches shall be in his house.

Fools make a mock at sin.

❁

If *I* provide not for *my* own, and specially for those of *my* own house,
I have denied the faith and am worse than an infidel.

❁

With the same measure that *I* mete, it shall be measured to *me* again.

❁

He that is faithful in that which is least is faithful also in much:
and he that is unjust in the least is unjust also in much.

❁

To whom much is given, of him shall be much required.

❁

I am the temple of God, and the Spirit of God dwells in *me*.
If *I* defile the temple of God, He shall destroy *me*.

❁

Grow in grace and in the knowledge of our Lord and Saviour Jesus Christ.
To Him be glory both now and forever.

❁

The smallest good deed is better than the grandest good intention.

meekness

God has two dwellings: one in heaven
and the other in a meek and thankful heart.

✿

A child may have more real wisdom
than a brilliant philosopher who does not know God.

✿

Meekness is surrendering to God.

✿

Though the Lord be high, He has respect unto the lowly.

✿

If I exalt myself, I shall be abased, if I humble myself, I shall be exalted.

✿

Humble yourself under the mighty Hand of God
and He will exalt you in due time.

✿

God resists the proud, but gives grace to the humble.

✿

When I think I stand, I should take heed lest I fall!

Before honor is humility.

✿

They that know God will be humble;
they that know themselves cannot be proud.

✿

Humility is a strange thing.
The minute you think you've got it, you've lost it.

✿

Learn from the mistakes of others—
you can't live long enough to make them all yourself.

✿

True greatness consists in being great in little things.

✿

What if the little rain should say,
"As small a drop as I
Can never refresh a drooping earth,
I'll tarry in the sky."

✿

Nothing is too small to play a part in God's scheme.

It is they who do their duties in every-day and trivial matters
who also fulfill them on great occasions.

❀

Everyone is ignorant—only on different subjects.

❀

God's strength is made perfect in weakness.

❀

An admission of error is a sign of strength
rather than a confession of weakness.

❀

When success turns a man's head, he is facing failure.

❀

To err may be human, but to admit isn't.

❀

I'd admit my faults, if I had any.

❀

It is better to understand a little
than to misunderstand a lot.

We may be taught by every person we meet.

❁

A man wrapped up in himself makes a very small bundle.

❁

The more you know, the more you know you don't know.

❁

Most people's hindsight is 20/20.

❁

It is no advantage for a man to know much
unless he lives according to what he knows.

❁

Nothing is done finally and right.

❁

Nothing is known positively and completely.

❁

A wise son makes a glad father.

❁

Children should hear the instruction of their parents.

The ways of man are before the eyes of the Lord,
and He ponders all his goings.

Receive with meekness the engrafted Word
which is able to save your soul.

God gives grace to the lowly.

A meek and quiet spirit is of great price in the sight of God.

Jesus came not to ministered unto, but to minister,
and to give His life a ransom for many.

In honor prefer one another.

Submit yourself to every ordinance of man for the Lord's sake
for so is the will of God.

If anyone asks you to go a mile, go with him two.

I am only one, but I am one.
I cannot do everything, but I can do something.

❀

Are you sure that you are Right?
How fine and strong!
But were you ever just as sure —
And wrong?

❀

The greatest truth are the simplest and so are the greatest men.

❀

A man's life does not consist in the abundance of things
which he possesses.

❀

I brought nothing into this world,
and it is certain I shall carry nothing out.

❀

The common people heard Jesus gladly.

❀

I am the clay, and God is the potter;
and I am the work of His Hand!

Whatsoever shall keep the commandments and teach them,
he shall be called great in the kingdom of heaven.

❁

Man shall not live by bread alone, but by every word
that proceeds out of the mouth of God.

❁

Let not the rich man glory in his riches.

❁

Glory only in the Lord.

❁

Every one of us shall give account of himself to God.
Let us not therefore judge one another.

❁

Dear Lord, Help me never to judge another
until I have walked two weeks in his shoes.

❁

God understands my thoughts afar off
and is acquainted with all my ways.
There is not a word in my tongue, but He knows it.

Boast not yourself of tomorrow;
for you know not what day may bring forth.

❁

I should say, if the Lord will, I shall live, and do this or that,
for I know not what shall be on the morrow.

❁

The Lord is near unto them that are of a broken heart;
and saves such as be of a contrite spirit.

❁

The Lord can mend my broken heart
if I give Him *all* the pieces.

❁

Love not the praise of men more than the praise of God.

❁

Let another man praise me and not my own mouth;
a stranger and not my own lips.

❁

Dear Lord, Let the words of my mouth and the meditation
of my heart be pleasing in Your sight.

Let not the wise man glory in his wisdom.

There is more hope for a fool than for a man wise in his own conceits.

I am not conceited, though I do have every reason to be.

God has chosen the foolish things of the world to confound the wise.

Let not the mighty man glory in his might.

God has chosen the weak things of the world
to confound the mighty.

A mighty man is not delivered by much strength.

The dewdrop, as the boundless sea
In God's great plan has part;
And this is all He asks of thee,
Be faithful, where thou art.

Meekness is not weakness.

❁

Humility is a kind of gratitude.

❁

Let the little children come unto Jesus:
for of such is the kingdom of heaven!

❁

Kindness is a language the dumb can speak and the deaf understand.

❁

I can be kind in looks, words and acts.

❁

Every deed of love and kindness done to man is done to God.

❁

One cannot find any rule of conduct to excel 'simplicity' and 'sincerity'.

❁

True nobility comes of the gentle heart.

❁

A gentleman is a gentle man.

Be kind one to another, tenderhearted,
forgiving one another even as God
for Christ's sake has forgiven you.

❁

Nothing will make us so kind and tender to the faults of others
as to thoroughly examine ourselves.

❁

Be kind, for everyone you meet is fighting a hard battle.

❁

Rejoice with them that do rejoice
and weep with them that weep.

❁

The merciful shall obtain mercy.

❁

He that has mercy on the poor, happy is he.

❁

A candle-glow can pierce the darkest night.

❁

Do you care for the poor at your door?

Be gentle to all people.

❊

We cannot always oblige, but we can always speak obligingly.

❊

The Lord is good and ready to forgive;
and plenteous in mercy unto all them who call upon Him.

❊

I have wept in the night for the shortness of sight
That to somebody's need made me blind;
But I never have yet felt a twinge of regret
For being a little too kind.

❊

The kindly word that falls today may bear its fruit tomorrow.

❊

The art of being kind is all this world needs.

❊

When we forgive ourselves and others, God will forgive us.

❊

A non-forgiving heart cannot be forgiven.

Forgiveness is the sweet smell the violet sheds
on the heel that crushed it.

❁

Nothing is so strong as gentleness
and nothing so gentle as real strength.

❁

The more perfect we are, the more gentle and quiet
we become toward the defects of others.

❁

The test of good manners is being able to
put up pleasantly with bad ones.

❁

Be to his virtues very kind—
Be to his faults a little blind.

❁

Disagree without being disagreeable.

❁

Punctuality is the politeness of kings
and the duty of gentle people everywhere.

True politeness is perfect ease and freedom; it simply consists
in treating others as you love to be treated yourself.

❀

A small unkindness is a great offense.

❀

Love ever gives and forgives.

❀

Few things are more bitter than to feel bitter.

❀

Talk to God as friend to friend.

❀

It takes two to quarrel and it takes two to make up after a quarrel.

❀

I really should be first to say hello—first to smile
—and, if necessary, first to forgive.

❀

If I am stronger than another,
I should do more for him than he does for me.

A good memory is fine—
but the ability to forget is the true test of greatness.

❁

Has someone drawn a circle and shut you out?
You and Love can outsmart him.
Draw a bigger circle and take him in.

❁

It is right that we remember wrongs done to us
so that we may forgive those who wronged us.

❁

It is in pardoning others that God pardons us.

❁

If you are not for yourself, who will be for you?

❁

If you are for yourself alone, then why are you?

❁

A smart alec is a person who thinks
he knows as much as I know I do.

Listening is a way of loving.

I was angry with my friend,
I told my wrath, my wrath did end.
I was angry with my foe;
I hid my wrath, my wrath did grow.

Maturity is humility. A mature person is able to say,
"I was wrong." He is also able to say, "I am sorry." And when
he is proven right, he does not have to say, "I told you so."

Little drops of water,
Little grains of sand,
Make the mighty ocean
And the pleasant land.

And the little moments,
Humble though they be,
Make the mighty ages
Of eternity.

Don't brag—it isn't the whistle that pulls the train.

Education is the process whereby one goes
from cocksure ignorance to thoughtful uncertainty.

❀

A humble, lowly, contrite heart,
Believing, true, and clean,
Which neither life nor death can part
From Him who dwells within.

❀

Be not like the cock who thought the sun rose to hear him crow.

❀

Meekness is that temper of spirit in which
we accept God's dealing with us as good.

❀

I can see my true significance only after I have realized my insignificance.

❀

There is no surer sign of perfection
than a willingness to be corrected.

❀

Humility is a lack of boastfulness or show of conceit.

Humility includes being kind and patient.

❁

O Hope of every contrite heart,
O Joy of all the meek,
To those who fall, how kind Thou art!
How good to those who seek!

❁

Humble yourselves in the sight of the Lord,
and he shall lift you up.

❁

Take a good look at yourself
and you will look at others differently.

❁

Humility is gratitude to God, the Giver of all good things.

❁

I shall never be deceived more by another than myself.

❁

If I would reflect upon what a small vacancy
my death would leave, I would not be inclined
to be too proud of my accomplishments.

God never makes me feel my weakness,
but that He may lead me to seek strength from Him.

❀

He gives power to the faint;
and to them that have no might he increases strength.

❀

Just as I am, I come to Thee, with my nothingness,
my wants, my sins and my contrition.

❀

If I will, I shall be taught;
and if I will apply my mind, I shall be prudent.

❀

You shall seek me, and find me,
when you shall search for me with all your heart.

❀

Dear Lord, help me to simplify everything.
May I walk in a plain, simple way and do the duty
closest to me, knowing the future is not mine.

❀

Mysteries are revealed unto the meek.

I know I am a weak image of my Lord
and a poor reflection of His goodness.
I also know any mercy I show comes from the Foundation of Mercy
and any love I show comes from God who is Love.

❀

May I be willing to help all and also be willing to be helped by all.

❀

Let me not be wise in my own eyes;
let me fear the Lord, and depart from evil.

❀

O, may my mind not be corrupted
from the simplicity that is in Christ.

❀

No evil happens to him that fears the Lord;
for God will deliver him in temptation.

❀

As for myself, I try to correct all the errors I make;
That's a high-minded goal, but a true one;
And I certainly never repeat a mistake—
No, I somehow come up with a new one.

We can't all be captains—some have to be crew.

❁

Win without boasting—lose without excuse.

❁

To me, to learn meekness is to learn
to trust in the Lord with all my heart
and lean not to my own understanding.

❁

When I come to my senses and find I have so little,
I get a taste of humility.

❁

My heart is open to those I love the best,
and therefore I cannot close my lips.

❁

True humility makes way for Christ
and throws the soul at His feet.

❁

Humility is the genuine proof of Christian virtue.
Never fear to admit your mistakes to your children.

The first test of a truly great person in his humility.
God walks with the humble;
He reveals Himself to the lowly.

The moment I think I am humble
is when I have lost my humility.
If I am truly humble, I will not think that I am humble.

The meek shall inherit the earth; and shall
delight themselves in the abundance of peace.

Life is a long lesson in humility.

I need the understanding of the heart
which is better than that of the head.

The first lesson in Christ's school is self-denial.

The very act of faith by which we receive Christ
is an act of utter renunciation of self.

Look not at the vices and imperfections of professing Christians.
Follow Jesus only as your example and you will learn
compassion for those who do not measure up to His standard.

Never underestimate the power of prayer.

For none of us lives to himself,
and no man dies to himself.

Take my yoke upon you, and learn of me;
for I am meek and lowly in heart:
and you shall find rest unto your souls.
For my yoke is easy, and my burden is light.

O, to be willing to change when wrong
and easy to live with when right!

What a small potato I am, compared with what I might be!

All I have is loaned to me by God.

Nothing is little in God's service.

❀

Commend not a man for his beauty; neither abhor a man
for his appearance. Man looks on the outward appearance,
but God looks upon the heart.

❀

At ten years of age a boy thinks his father knows a great deal.
At fifteen years of age he thinks he knows as much as his father.
At age twenty he knows twice as much as his father.
At age thirty he may accept advice from his father.
At age forty he begins to think his father knew something after all.
At age fifty he begins to seek advice from his father.
At age sixty when his father is dead and gone he thinks that Dad
was just about the smartest man that ever lived.

❀

After crosses and losses we become humble and wise.

❀

Nothing sets a person so much
out of the devil's reach as humility.

❀

To realize I am a sinner is the first step toward my salvation.

The person who lives by himself and for himself
is apt to be corrupted by the company he keeps.

❁

Life is a gift from God, and a Christian learns
to enjoy it to the highest degree.

❁

May each of us take up our tasks for the glory of God.
Then we may go to sleep, knowing that no one
could have done the job better than we tried to do it this day.

❁

Live virtuously and you will have no regrets.

❁

It is possible to profit by our errors
and derive experience from our folly.

❁

Nothing so well becomes true beauty as simplicity.

❁

Blessed are they which do hunger and thirst
after righteousness: for they shall be filled.

Life is a splendid gift.
To live my life I must discipline it.

❀

The blossom cannot tell what becomes of its scent, and
no person can tell what becomes of the influence and example
that roll away from him and go beyond his view.

❀

God loves us so much that He gave us laws to live by—
laws which, if we would obey, would make us happy.
He didn't give these laws to us to keep us from doing something,
to thwart us, to bind us, to hold us down, but that we might
live our lives to the fullest—as a river at flood stage or as a horse
running at full gallop, happy, bubbling over. He gave us the bible
that our joy might be full. Jesus came that we might have the more
abundant life. We are so blind to this truth and to the beauty
all around us, above us and at our feet. Call that your own
which no person can take from you. I may not own an inch of land,
but all I see is mine! Life is not a place of entertainment, and
youth and health and riches are not the highest attainments of life.

❀

I cannot run away from my weakness.
I must fight it out to victory or perish. If not now, when?

Too much noise deafens us. Too much light blinds us.
Standing back too far or up too close prevents our seeing.

❀

Health, beauty, vigor, riches and other good things
operate equally as evils to the unjust as they do benefits to the just.

❀

We are creatures of habit.
We succeed or we fail as we acquire good habits or bad ones.

❀

Take care to economize in prosperity,
you will have to in adversity.

❀

Gain and income may be temporary and uncertain,
but expenses are constant and certain.

❀

No one is poor whose incomings exceed his outgoings.

❀

Saving money soon grows to yield more pleasure
than careless spending.

The choicest pleasures of life lie
within the ring of moderation.

❁

If I keep my mouth and tongue,
I keep my soul from troubles.

❁

Death and life are in the power of the tongue.

❁

He that refrains his lips is wise.

❁

If I will incline my ear unto wisdom, and apply my heart
to understanding; if I cry after knowledge, and lift up my voice
for understanding; if I seek wisdom like I would search for gold
and silver and hidden treasures; then I will understand
the fear of the Lord and find the knowledge of God.

❁

It is the lord who gives wisdom; out of His mouth comes
knowledge and understanding. When wisdom enters into my
heart, and knowledge is pleasant to my soul, then discretion
shall preserve me, and understanding shall keep me.

When God would educate a man, He compels him to learn better lessons.
He sends him to school to learn the necessities rather than the graces,
that by knowing all suffering, he may also know the eternal consolation.

❀

I cannot conquer fate and necessity, but I can yield to them
in such a manner as to be greater than if I could.

❀

I may not be able to change my circumstances,
but I can change my attitude toward them.

❀

It is true that earth might be fair and all men glad and wise,
but it isn't always.

❀

Meekness, temperance: against such there is no law.

❀

I have learned, in whatsoever state I am, to be content.
I know both how to be abased, and I know how to abound;
every where and in all things I am instructed both to be full
and to be hungry, both to abound and to suffer need.
I can do all things through Christ which strengthens me.

The fear of the Lord is the beginning of wisdom;
and the knowledge of the holy is understanding.

❁

Happy are they who find wisdom, and they who get understanding.
For the merchandise of it is better than the merchandise of silver,
and the gain thereof than fine gold. She is more precious than rubies;
and all the things I can desire are not to be compared unto her.
Length of days is in her right hand; and in her left hand riches and honor.
Her ways are the ways of pleasantness, and all her paths are peace.
She is a tree of life to them that lay hold upon her:
and happy is every one that retains her.

❁

Riches and honor are with wisdom and righteousness.

❁

When wisdom enters into my heart,
and knowledge is pleasant to *my* soul;
discretion shall preserve *me*,
understanding shall keep *me*.

❁

How much better is it to get wisdom than gold!
and to get understanding rather than silver!

Wisdom is better than strength: nevertheless the poor man's
wisdom is despised, and his words are not heard.
The words of wise men are heard in quiet more than
the cry of him that rules among fools. Wisdom is better
than weapons of war: but one sinner destroys much good.

There is more hope for a fool than for a man wise in his own conceits.

Understanding is a wellspring of life for him who has it.

Better is a poor and wise child than an old and foolish king
who will no more be admonished.

God gives to a man that is good in His sight
wisdom, and knowledge, and joy.

It is better for *me* to hear the rebuke of the wise,
than for *me* to hear the song of fools.

A man's life consists not in the abundance of things which he possesses.

Every man also to whom God has given riches and wealth,
and has given him power to eat thereof, and to take his portion,
and to rejoice in his labor; this is the gift of God.

❀

There are those that make themselves rich, and yet have nothing:
there are those that make themselves poor, yet have great riches.

❀

Wealth gotten by vanity shall be diminished;
but he that gathers by labor shall increase.

❀

He becomes poor that deals with a slack hand;
but the hand of the diligent makes rich.

❀

I am a fool if *I* lay up treasure for *myself*,
and am not rich toward God.

❀

Better is little with fear of the Lord
than great treasure and trouble therein.

❀

Learn to be content in whatsoever state *you* are.

Take no thought for *your* life, what you shall eat;
neither for the body, what you shall put on.
The life is more than meat, and the body is more than raiment.

A good name is rather to be chosen than great riches,
and loving favor rather than silver and gold.

Two are better than one; because they have a good reward for their labor.
If they fall, the one will lift up his fellow: but woe to him that is alone
when he falls; for he has not another to help him up.

He who sows sparingly shall reap also sparingly;
and he who sows bountifully shall reap also bountifully.

But rather seek the kingdom of God;
and all these things shall be added unto you.

So teach *me* to number *my* days, that *I* may apply *my* heart unto wisdom.

The words of a wise man's mouth are gracious.

A little that a righteous man has
is better than the riches of many wicked.

❁

Righteousness exalts a nation; but sin is a reproach to any people.

❁

By much slothfulness the building decays;
and through the idleness of the hands the house falls down.

❁

Pleasant words are as a honeycomb, sweet to the soul,
and health to the bones.

❁

A merry heart does good like a medicine.

❁

The lips of the righteous feed many: but fools die for want of wisdom.

❁

The fear of the Lord is the instruction of wisdom;
and before honor is humility.

❁

A word fitly spoken is like apples of gold in pictures of silver.

Even so the tongue is a little member, and boasts great things.
Behold, how great a matter a little fire kindles!

Even a fool, when he holds his peace, is counted wise:
and he who shuts his lips is esteemed a man of understanding.

… Aged men be sober, grave, temperate,
sound in faith, in charity, in patience.
The aged women likewise… that they may teach the young women
to be sober, to love their husbands, to love their children.

If *I* correct my son, he shall give *me* rest;
yes, he shall give delight unto *my* soul.

Children's children are the crown of old men;
and the glory of children are their fathers.

Children should hear the instruction of their parents.

My son, give God your heart, and let your eyes observe His ways.

A wise son makes a glad father:
but a foolish son despises his mother.

❀

Forsake not mercy and truth,... then shall *you* find favor
and good understanding in the sight of God and man.

❀

Abstain from all appearance of evil.

❀

If *I* give, it shall be given to *me*, good measure, pressed down,
and shaken together and running over.

❀

A merry heart makes a cheerful countenance:
but by sorrow of the heart the spirit is broken.

❀

The judgments of the Lord are true and righteous.
More to be desired are they than gold,
sweeter also than honey and the honeycomb.

❀

I shall give account, in the day of judgment,
of every idle word *I* speak.

The Lord is near unto them that are of a broken heart;
and saves such as be of a contrite spirit.

❀

Man shall not live by bread alone,
but by every word that proceeds out of the mouth of God.

❀

He who covers a transgression seeks love;
but he who repeats a matter separates very friends.

❀

Hatred stirs up strifes: but love covers all sins.

❀

If the whole body were an eye, where were the hearing?
If the whole were hearing, where were the smelling?...
God has set every member in the body as it has pleased Him...
If one member suffers, all the members suffer with it.

❀

God has created all things,
and for His pleasure they are and were created.

❀

The Lord is good to all: and His tender mercies are over all His works.

Whatsoever things are true,
Whatsoever things are honest,
Whatsoever things are just,
Whatsoever things are pure,
Whatsoever things are lovely,
Whatsoever things are of good report;
if there be any virtue,
and if there be any praise,
think on these things.

The Lord is merciful and gracious, slow to anger,
and plenteous in mercy.

Christ suffered for *me*, leaving *me* an example,
that *I* should follow in His steps.

❀

Let us bear one another's burdens,
and so fulfil the law of Christ.

❀

Create in *me* a clean heart, O God;
and renew a right spirit within *me*.

He who follows after righteousness and mercy
finds life, righteousness and honor.

❁

Withhold not good from them to whom it is due,
when it is in the power of *your* hand to do it.

❁

Cast out the beam from *your* own eye; and *you* shall see clearly
to cast out the mote out of *your* brother's eye.

❁

Strive not about words to no profit.

❁

Love your enemies, do good to them that hate *you*…
that you may be children of *your* Father which is in heaven:
for He makes His sun to shine on the evil and on the good,
and sends rain on the just and the unjust.

❁

The spirit Itself bears witness with *my* spirit,
that *I* am a child of God.

❁

Be holy in all manner of conversation.

The wisdom that is from above is first pure,
then peaceable, gentle, and easy to be intreated, full of mercy
and good fruits, without partiality, and without hypocrisy.

❁

Strive not; but be gentle unto all men, apt to teach, patient,
in meekness instructing those who oppose themselves.

❁

Be still, and know that I am God.

❁

A soft answer turns away wrath:
but grievous words stir up anger.

❁

He who oppresses the poor reproaches his Maker:
but he who honors Him has mercy on the poor.

❁

Speak no evil of no man, be no brawler, but gentle,
showing all meekness to all men.

❁

A righteous man regards the life of his beast:
but the tender mercies of the wicked are cruel.

Be kind one to another, tenderhearted, forgiving one another,
even as God has forgiven you.

❀

Avoid foolish and unlearned questions, knowing they are gender strife.

❀

Let not the sun go down on *your* wrath.

❀

A repoof means more to a wise man than a hundred stripes to a fool.

❀

All things are lawful for *me*,… but all things edify not.

❀

All things whatsoever *I* would that men should do to *me*,
I must do even so to them.

❀

I am inexcusable if *I* judge another,
… for *I* that judge, do the same things.

❀

God's mercy is on them who fear Him
from generation to generation.

The Lord daily loads *me* with benefits.

❀

God shall give His angels charge over *me*, to keep *me*
in all *my* ways. They shall bear *me* up in their hands,
lest *I* dash *my* foot against a stone.

❀

O Lord, save *me* for Thy mercies' sake.

❀

Love not the praise of men more than the praise of God.

❀

Favor is deceitful, and beauty is vain;
but a woman that fears the Lord, she shall be praised.
Give her of the fruit of her hands; and let her own works praise her.

❀

All the paths of the Lord are mercy and truth
unto such as keep His covenant and His testimonies.

❀

Cease from anger, and forsake wrath.

He that has mercy on the poor, happy is he.

❂

The pure in heart shall see God.

❂

The merciful shall obtain mercy.

❂

Suffer the little children to come unto Jesus:
for of such is the kingdom of heaven.

❂

It were better for *me* that a millstone were hanged about *my* neck,
and that *I* were drowned in the bottom of the sea,
than that *I* should offend a little one.

❂

With the merciful God will show Himself merciful;
with an upright man He will show Himself upright;
with the pure He will show Himself pure.

❂

It is more blessed to give than to receive.

I have been given exceeding great and precious promises,
by which *I* may be a partaker of the divine nature.

❁

If *I* say *I* abide in Jesus, *I* should walk even as He walked.

❁

Father, forgive them; for they know not what they do.

❁

Goodness and mercy shall follow *me* all the days of *my* life:
and *I* will dwell in the house of the Lord for ever.

❁

The fruit of the Spirit is love, joy, peace, longsuffering, gentleness,
goodness, faith, meekness and temperance.

❁

Add to *your* faith virtue; and to virtue knowledge;
and to knowledge temperance; and to temperance patience;
and to patience godliness; and to godliness brotherly kindness;
and to brotherly kindness charity.

❁

Though the Lord be high, yet has He respect unto the lowly.

If these things be in *me*, and abound, *I* shall neither be barren
nor unfruitful in the knowledge of our Lord Jesus Christ.
If *I* lack these things, *I* am blind, and cannot see afar off
and have forgotten that *I* was purged from *my* old sins.

Fear *you* not Me? says the Lord; will *you* not tremble at My presence,
Who has placed the sand for the bound of the sea by a perpetual decree,
that it cannot pass it: and though the waves thereof toss themselves, yet
can they not prevail; though they roar, yet can they not pass over it?

Thus says the high and lofty One that inhabits eternity,
Whose name is Holy: I dwell in the high and holy place, with
him also that is of a contrite and humble spirit, to revive the spirit
of the humble, and to revive the heart of the contrite ones.

God is the judge: He puts down one and sets up another.

When *you* pray, do not use vain repetitions…
for *your* Father knows what things *you* have need of,
before *you* ask Him.

Humble *yourself* in the sight of the Lord,
and He will lift *you* up.

✿

God resists the proud, but gives grace to the humble.

✿

The Lord is gracious, and full of compassion;
slow to anger, and of great mercy.

✿

Humble *yourself* under the mighty hand of God
and He will exalt *you* in due time.

✿

When *I* think *I* stand, *I* should take heed lest *I* fall.

✿

Everyone one of us shall give account of himself to God.
Let us not therefore judge one another any more.

✿

One day is with the Lord as a thousand years,
and a thousand years as one day.

When *you* give *your* alms, do not sound a trumpet before you,
as the hypocrites do… that they may have glory from men.

The Lords lift up the meek.

If *I* exalt *myself,* *I* shall be abased, if *I* humble *myself,* *I* shall be exalted.

God knows *my* downsitting and *my* uprising, He understands
my thoughts afar off and is acquainted with all *my* ways.
There is not a word in *my* tongue, but He knows it.

Boast not *yourself* of tomorrow;
for *you* know not what a day may bring forth.

God forgets not the cry of the humble.

To every thing there is a season, and a time
to every purpose under the heaven.

God raises up the poor... that He may set him with princes.

❁

Every one that is proud in heart is an abomination to the Lord.

❁

The ways of man are before the eyes of the Lord,
and He ponders all his goings.

❁

God gives grace to the lowly.

❁

Submit *yourself* to every ordinance of man for the Lord's sake,
for so is the will of God.

❁

For the Lord takes pleasure in His people:
He will beautify the meek with salvation.

❁

Jesus came not to be ministered unto, but to minister,
and to give His life a ransom for many.

❁

Be in the fear of the Lord all day long.

Whosoever shall do the commandments and teach them,
he shall be called great in the kingdom of heaven.

❂

Be kindly affectioned one to another with brotherly love;
in honor preferring one another.

❂

There is no man that has power over the spirit to retain the spirit;
neither has he power in the day of death.

❂

By humility and the fear of the Lord are riches, and honor, and life.

❂

When pride comes, then comes shame:
but with the lowly is wisdom.

❂

There is a way which seems right unto a man,
but the end thereof are the ways of death.

❂

The natural man receives not the things of the Spirit of God;
for they are foolishness unto him: neither can he know them,
because they are spiritually discerned.

God's thoughts are not *my* thoughts,
neither are *my* ways His ways, says the Lord.

❁

Woe unto them that are wise in their own eyes,
and prudent in their own sight!

❁

The entrance of God's word gives light;
it gives understanding to the simple.

❁

Receive with meekness the engrafted word,
which is able to save *your* soul.

❁

There are diversities of gifts, but the same Spirit.
There are differences of administrations, but the same Lord. There are
diversities of operations, but it is the same God Who works all in all.

❁

I am the clay, and God is the potter; and *I* am the work of His hand.

❁

Let another man praise you and not your own mouth;
a stranger and not your own lips.

Let the words of *my* mouth and the meditation of *my* heart,
be acceptable in your sight, O Lord, *my* strength, and *my* redeemer.

❀

Be subject one to another, and be clothed with humility:
for God resists the proud, and gives grace to the humble.

❀

If any man desire to be first, the same shall be last of all,
and servant of all.

❀

Pride goes before destruction, and an haughty spirit before a fall.

❀

He, who being often reproved and hardens his neck,
shall suddenly be destroyed, and that without remedy.

❀

God's goodness and forbearance and longsuffering
should lead *me* to repentance.

❀

I brought nothing into this world,
and it is certain *I* shall carry nothing out.

Let not the wise man glory in his wisdom,
neither let the mighty man glory in his might,
let not the rich man glory in his riches:
but let him that glories glory in this,
that he understands and knows me,
that I am the Lord which exercise lovingkindness,
judgment, and righteousness, in the earth:
for in these things I delight, says the Lord.

❁

The sacrifices of God are a broken spirit:
a broken and a contrite heart, O God, You will not despise.

❁

God's strength is made perfect in weakness.

❁

The meek shall inherit the earth;
and shall delight themselves in the abundance of peace.

❁

A meek and quiet spirit is of great price in the sight of God.

❁

If *I* think that *I* know anything,
I know nothing yet as *I* ought to know.

patience

Genius is only patience.

❀

Life is 10 percent what you make it and 90 percent how you take it.

❀

There is no failure save in giving up.

❀

We can do most anything we want if we stick to it long enough.

❀

If you never stick your neck out,
you'll never get your head above the crowd.

❀

Forget mistakes. Organize victory out of mistakes.

❀

A man can fail many times, but he isn't a failure
until he begins to blame somebody else.

❀

The greatest calamity is not to have failed;
but to have failed to try.

The only time you mustn't fail
is the last time you try.

❁

Only one person in the whole wide world can defeat you.
That is yourself.

❁

We cannot do everything at once;
but we can do something at once.

❁

A mistake is evidence
that someone has tried to do something.

❁

Trying times are times for trying.

❁

Trouble is only opportunity in work clothes.

❁

The difference between stumbling blocks and
stepping-stones is the way we use them.

The secret of patience is doing something else
in the meantime.

❊

Sometimes the best gain is to lose.

❊

Mastery in any art comes only with long practice.

❊

A little more determination, a little more pluck,
a little more work—that's LUCK.

❊

Difficulties strengthen the mind, as labor does the body.

❊

I will not fail unless I give up trying.

❊

Failing is not falling, but in failing to rise when you fall.

❊

You may if you try—You won't if you don't.

If at first you don't succeed, you are running about average.

❀

The burdens don't matter
as long as I remember to give them to God.

❀

No difficulties, no discovery.

❀

No pains, no gain.

❀

The more difficult the obstacle,
the stronger one becomes after hurdling it.

❀

The secret of success is hard work.

❀

Education is hard, hard work, b
ut it can be made interesting work.

❀

The grass may seem greener on the other side,
but it is just as hard to mow.

A smooth sea never made a skillful mariner.

❁

The dictionary is the only place where success comes before work.

❁

The quitter never wins.

❁

The winner never quits.

❁

You can't slide uphill.

❁

An ounce of pluck is worth a ton of luck.

❁

If at first you do succeed, try something harder.

❁

Experience is what makes you wonder
how it got a reputation for being the best teacher.

❁

When you begin to coast you know you are on the downgrade.

It does one good to be somewhere parched by the heat
and drenched by the rain of life.

To find fault is easy; to do better may be difficult.

Shoot at everything and hit nothing.

Make haste slowly.

Pure gold can lie for a month in the furnace without losing a grain.

It isn't the mountain ahead that wears you out—
it's the grain of sand in your shoe.

Instead of waiting upon the Lord,
some people want the Lord to wait upon them.

Every time you give another a "piece of your mind,"
you add to your own vacuum.

The night is not forever.

❀

Itching for what you want doesn't do much good;
you've got to scratch for it.

❀

If all men are created equal,
it is because they have 24 hours a day.

❀

It is easier to be critical than correct.

❀

Firmness is that admirable quality in ourselves
that is merely stubbornness in others.

❀

Pay to no one evil for evil.

❀

Be not weary in well doing.

❀

Overcome evil with good.

Be patient with everyone.

❀

Murmor not.

❀

If you can't have the best of everything,
make the best of everything you have.

❀

The man who rows the boat doesn't have time to rock it.

❀

Do the truth you know and you shall learn the truth you need to know.

❀

Before you flare up at anyones faults,
take time to count ten—ten of your own.

❀

There's no sense in advertising your troubles.
There is no market for them.

❀

Why value the present hour less than some future hour?

Telling your troubles always helps. The world's dumb indifference
makes you mad enough to keep on trying.

If you don't scale the mountain, you can't see the view.

It isn't the load that weighs us down—
it's the way we carry it.

Let us then, be up and doing
With a heart for any fate,
Still achieving, still pursuing,
Learn to labor and to wait.

The late blooming virtues can be the very best.

Life is hard by the yard—By the inch, it's a cinch.

When God makes an oak tree, he takes 20 years.
He takes only two months to make a squash.

The diamond cannot be polished without friction,
nor man perfected without trials.

❀

The aim of education is to teach us how to think,
not what to think.

❀

Instruction may end in the schoolroom,
but education ends only with life.

❀

Character development is the true aim of education.

❀

One learns manners from those who have none.

❀

Were I chaste as ice and pure as snow,
I should not escape slander.

❀

You are only young once,
but you can stay immature almost indefinitely.

When you are through changing, you're through.

Age has many blessings youth cannot understand.

Will Power! Won't Power! Supreme Power!

Habit is a cable; we weave a thread of it every day;
and at last we cannot break it.

We first make our habits, and then our habits make us.

The chains of habit are generally too small to be felt
until they are too strong to be broken.

Habit, if not resisted, soon becomes necessity.

Everything comes to him who waits,
if he works while he waits.

One thing at a time and that done well
Is a very good rule—as many can tell.

❊

Housework is something you do that nobody notices
unless you don't do it.

❊

God never makes us conscious of our weakness
except to give us of His strength.

❊

Anytime a person takes a stand, there'll come a time
when he'll be tested to see how firm his feet are planted.

❊

Poise is the art of raising the eyebrows instead of the roof.

❊

Don't lessen the lesson.

❊

He surely is most in need of another's patience who has none of his own.

❊

No one is as old as he hopes to be.

No wise man ever wished to be younger.

A stitch in time saves nine.

Better to slip with the foot than with the tongue.

Better let them wonder why you didn't talk
than why you did.

Habits are first cobwebs, then cables.

Commit a sin twice, and it will seem no longer a sin.

Habit can be my best friend or my worst enemy.

A loose tongue often gets into a tight place.

Is it true? Is it necessary? Will it help?

Use speech for spreading good will.

❀

He who keeps his mouth and his tongue keeps his soul from troubles.

❀

He that can rule his tongue shall live without strife.

❀

A fool utters all in his mind; but a wise man keeps it in till afterwards.

❀

It's all right to hold a conversation,
but you should let go of it now and then.

❀

Even a fool, when he holds his peace, is counted wise.

❀

He that has knowledge spares his words.

❀

He that refrains his lips is wise.

❀

In a multitude of words there lacks not sin.

I shall give account on the day of judgment
for every idle word I speak.

I have often regretted my speech, seldom my silence.

Tact is the ability to close your mouth before someone else wants to.

Think all you speak, but speak not all you think.

Nothing is opened more by mistake than the mouth.

Best rule I know for talking is the same as the one for carpentering—
Measure twice and saw once.

Brevity is the soul of wit and even wit is a burden
when it talks too long.

They think too little who talk too much.

Some people need a double chin.
There's too much work for one.

❋

We weaken what we exaggerate.

❋

Listening is wanting to hear.

❋

A good listener is not only popular everywhere,
but after a while he knows something.

❋

Tact is the unsaid part of what you think.

❋

Words in haste do friendships waste.

❋

'A soft answer turns away wrath'
is the best system of self-defense.

❋

Who gossips to you will gossip of you.

When music speaks, all other voices should cease.

❀

Taste your words before you let them pass your teeth.

❀

Do not say a little in many words, but a great deal in a few.

❀

The longer you keep your temper,
the more it will improve.

❀

Silence is not always golden—sometimes it is just plain yellow.

❀

Set a watch, O Lord, before my mouth; keep the door of my lips.
Let me say the right things rightly.

❀

Temper, if ungoverned, governs the whole person.

❀

When angry count ten before you speak;
if very angry, count a hundred.

Let not the sun go down upon your wrath.

❁

He who can suppress a moment's anger
may prevent a day of sorrow.

❁

Swallowing your pride occasionally
will never give you indigestion.

❁

A small leak will sink a great ship.

❁

People who fly into a rage always make a bad landing.

❁

There are times when nothing a man can say
is nearly so powerful as saying nothing.

❁

It is easy to dodge an elephant but not a fly.

❁

The gliding of the key will not make it open the door better.

Your body is for use—not abuse.

❁

Dope is for dopes.

❁

Think: Will this turn me on or will it turn on me?

❁

Work is the best narcotic.

❁

The key to a lot of troubles is the one that fits the ignition.

❁

Statistics prove folk who drive like crazy are.

❁

The first step in making a dream come true is to wake up.

❁

A college graduate is a person
who had a chance to get an education.

❁

As easy as falling off a diet.

Will power is the ability to eat one salted peanut.

❀

The archer who overshoots his mark
does no better than he who falls short of it.

❀

Do you act or react?

❀

There's a slight difference between keeping your chin up
and sticking your neck out, but it's worth knowing.

❀

Taste makes waist.

❀

Laziness travels so slowly that poverty soon overtakes him.

❀

Thrift is a wonderful virtue—especially in ancestors.

❀

Spend less than you get.

A penny saved is as good as a penny earned.

❁

Waste not, want not.

❁

Willful waste makes woeful want.

❁

Stretching the truth won't make it last any longer.

❁

If I know enough to do a thing, I know enough not to do a thing.

❁

Don't tell your friends about your indigestion:
'How are you' is a greeting, not a question.

❁

Prejudice is being down on what we are not up on.

❁

If you blame others for your failures,
do you credit others with your successes?

Old-timers who recall the hip-deep snows
of their childhood should remember that when
they were children their hips were lower.

❀

To sin by silence when they should protest, makes cowards of men.

❀

If you have a weakness, make it work for you as a strength—
and if you have a strength, don't abuse it into a weakness.

❀

Somebody thought Anybody would do it,
and Somebody thought Everybody should.
Guess who finally did it? That's right—Nobody.

❀

Everybody's business is nobody's business.

❀

Wouldn't it be nice if we could find other things
as easily as we find fault?

❀

God has a song to teach us, and when we have learned it
amid the shadows of affliction, we can sing it forever.

A man shows what he is by what he does with what he has.

Good timber does not grow in ease,
The stronger wind, the stronger trees;
The farther sky, the greater length,
The more the storms, the more the strength.
By sun and cold, by rain and snow,
In tree or man good timber grows.

Many of the things that go wrong surprise us by turning out all right.

More people would be on Easy Street if they were willing
to go through a tough neighborhood to get there.

❀

The greatest and sublimest power is often simple patience.

❀

The cloud that darkens the present hour may brighten all our future days.

❀

Free enterprise gives everybody a chance to get to the top.
Some depend on the free and not enough on the enterprise.

Not so in haste, my heart,
Have faith in God and wait:
Although He lingers very long,
He never comes too late.

God never comes too late,
He knows what is best.
Vex not thyself today in vain,
Until He comes, I rest.

❁

Dear Lord, Help me never to judge another
until I have walked two weeks in his shoes.

❁

To err is human—and sometimes it is the best thing
that could happen to us.

❁

Tomorrow is still untouched.

❁

Take me, break me, mold me to the pattern You have planned for me.

❁

In quietness and in confidence shall be your strength.

Must I be carried to the skies
On flowery beds of ease,
While others fought to win the prize,
And sailed through bloody seas?

My soul with patience waits
For You, the living Lord;
My hopes are on Your promise built,
Your never failing Word.

❋

If you would suffer patiently the adversities and
miseries of this life, be a person of prayer.

❋

Love and wait!

❋

Anxiety does not empty tomorrow of its worries and sorrows,
but it helps to empty today of its strength.

❋

I refuse to be disquieted by trifles.

❋

Cast all your care upon him; for he cares for you.

A childlike trust in God is the best preventative
and remedy for anxiety.

❀

When through the deep waters God calls me to go,
The rivers of sorrow shall not overflow.
For He will be with me my trials to bless
And sanctify to me my deepest distress.

When through fiery trials my pathway shall lie,
His grace all sufficient shall be my supply.
The flame shall not hurt me,
He only designs my dross to consume
And my gold to refine.

My soul, though all hell should endeavor to shake,
He'll never, no, never, no never forsake!

❀

I am content, to know that all my times are in God's hand.
I cast all my care upon Him, and I doubt not that the anchor shall hold.

❀

If I learn to adjust to changing circumstances and remain at peace,
then a wind that would blow me off course
will instead blow me into port even earlier.

See God in all places, all things, all events at all times.

❁

A heart that worships God alone
and trusts Him rises above anxiety.

❁

Complete faith in God puts anxiety to rest.

❁

This shaking world need not shake the Christian's composure.

❁

Why should this anxious load
Press down my weary mind?
I'll hasten to my heavenly Father's throne
And sweet refreshment find.

❁

Murmur not at the ills you may suffer,
but rather thank God for the many mercies and blessings
you have received at His hand.

❁

For you have need of endurance, so that you may do
the will of God and receive what is promised.

God has a song to teach us, and when we have learned it
amid the shadows of affliction, we can sing it forever.

❂

Whatsoever things were written aforetime
were written for our learning, that we through patience
and comfort of the scriptures might have hope.

❂

A man has to do his own growing
no matter how tall his father was.

❂

Better is the end of a thing than the beginning
and the patient in spirit is better than the proud in spirit.

❂

"The good old days" were once called "these trying times."

❂

It is good that a man should both hope and quietly wait
for the salvation of the Lord.

❂

Only I can fill my place in the world.

I take with solemn thankfulness
My burden up, nor ask it less,
And count it joy that even I
May suffer, serve, or wait for You,
Whose will be done.

The servant of the Lord must not strive;
but be gentle unto all men, apt to teach, patient.

If I have longed for shelter in Your fold
When You have given me some fort to hold.
Dear Lord, forgive.

The Lord will perfect that which concerns me:
His mercy endures for ever.

I practice the presence of God, for I know that He gives me
the very breath with which to praise Him and that I could not
even deny Him unless He gave me the breath to do so.

Very often the chip on a person's shoulder is just bark.

Patience is the ability to count down, before blasting off.

❁

He that is slow to anger is better than the mighty.

❁

Patience is the ability to idle your motor
when you feel like stripping your gears.

❁

You may not be required to finish the task,
but you are not permitted to lay it down.

❁

Let us, then, be up and doing
With a heart for any fate;
Still achieving, still pursuing,
Learn to labor and to wait.

❁

Patience is bitter, but its fruit is sweet.

❁

Every man that strives for mastery
is temperate in all things.

Like plants and trees, we grow spiritually
not only in sunshine, but in rain, wind, lightning,
thunder, hail and, yes, even in the earthquake.

❁

In the adversity and darkness of our lives we sometimes see lights
which were invisible to us when our lives were all sunshine.

❁

Let patience have her perfect work in all your griefs and trouble.

❁

In time all heaven will break loose.

❁

God upholds us in all our sorrows and is also able to do us good by them.

❁

No contrary wind can last forever.

❁

God permits trials and temptations to come to me
only for my own good or for the good of others.

❁

The trying of faith works patience.

The rains will fall, the winds will blow,
so we dare not build on the shifting sands.

❋

Love grows in us, and we grow in love.

❋

The tallest tree catches the most wind.

❋

The buds swell imperceptibly, without hurry or confusion,
as if the short spring days were an eternity.

❋

Experience is the Lord's school and we who are taught by Him
usually learn by the mistakes we make.

❋

Dear Lord, remind me often that I will not live long enough
to make all the mistakes.

❋

They that wait upon the Lord shall renew their strength;
they shall mount up with wings as eagles; they shall run,
and not be weary; and they shall walk, and not faint.

You cannot put the same shoe on every foot.

We do the difficult immediately—
the impossible takes a little longer.

Hurry is good for catching flies.

When an archer misses his mark,
he seeks for the cause within himself.

Parents should not expect horse and buggy notions
out of jet-age kids.

Only the best behavior is good enough
for daily use in the home.

My neighbor's little boy is confused.
Everytime his Mama gets worn out he has to take a nap.

Any woman who is married to a man who thinks he is smarter
than his wife is surely married to some smart woman.

❁

When you get to the "end of the rope," tie a knot in it and hang on.
This is just another way of saying, "Wait upon the Lord."

❁

Wait on the Lord: be of good courage,
and he shall strengthen your heart: wait, I say, on the Lord.

❁

All fathers, mothers and teachers
have the opportunity to train children.

❁

Patience is active. It is concentrated strength.
To learn to wait is a great secret of success.

❁

Learn to take life just as it blows.
Work and trust and wait.

❁

A great work requires a great and careful training.

Let us run with patience the race that is set before us.

❁

God is still trying to teach me that listening
is the most important part of the conversation.

❁

The Lord disciplines those whom He loves,
and chastises those whom He receives.

❁

Better is the end of a thing than the beginning thereof:
and the patient in spirit is better than the proud in spirit.

❁

Have mercy upon *me*, O God,
according to Your lovingkindness:
according to the multitude of Your tender mercies
blot out *my* transgressions.

❁

Bless the Lord, O *my* soul,
and forget not all His benefits:
Who forgives all *my* iniquities;
who heals all *my* diseases.

Why am *I* cast down, and why am *I* disquieted within?
I shall hope in God and shall yet praise Him,
Who is the health of *my* countenance.

❁

God heals the broken in heart, and binds up their wounds.

❁

We all need more patience,
though it does seem to me that the more I have,
the more my family wants to use.

❁

The best school of discipline is home.

❁

Boys will be boys and boys will grow up to be men.
As the twig is bent, the tree is inclined.
Of all the graces parents need, surely patience heads the list.
If necessary, tell your child a thousand times, "Close the door,
wash your hands, brush your teeth, study your lessons."

❁

Every word spoken in the hearing of little children
tends toward the formation of the character.

Education does not commence with the alphabet.
It begins with a mother's look, with a father's nod of approbation,
or a sign of reproof; with a sister's gentle pressure of the hand,
or a brother's noble act of forbearance.

There are months (perhaps years) between seedtime and harvest,
and the acorn does not become an oak in a day.

In *my* distress *I* called to the Lord, and cried to *my* God:
He heard *my* voice,… and *my* cry came before Him,
even into His ears.

The rock of *my* strength, and *my* refuge, is in God.

Despise the chastening of the Lord;
nor be weary of His correction:
for whom the Lord loves He corrects;
even as a father the song in whom he delights.

As many as God loves, He rebukes and chastens.

For a small moment has God forsaken *me*;
but with great mercies will He gather *me*.
In a little wrath He hid His face from *me* for a moment;
but with everlasting kindness will He have mercy on *me*,
says the Lord *my* Redeemer.

❀

When *I* pass through the waters, God will be with *me*;
and through the rivers, they shall not overflow *me*,
when *I* walk through the fire, *I* shall not be burned;
neither shall the flame kindle upon *me*.

❀

Take refuge in the shadow of God's wings
until *your* calamities are overpast.

❀

God has not despised nor abhorred the affliction of the afflicted;
neither has He hid His face from him;
but when he cried unto God, He heard.

❀

The salvation of the righteous is of the Lord:
He is their strength in the time of trouble.

The Lord also will be a refuge for the oppressed,
a refuge in times of trouble.

❂

I must through much tribulation enter into the kingdom of God.

❂

He that endures to the end shall be saved.

❂

He will regard the prayer of the destitute,
and not despise their prayer.

❂

We glory in tribulations also:
knowing that tribulation works patience;
And patience, experience; and experience, hope.

❂

Be patient toward all men.

❂

A prophet is not without honor, but in his own country,
and among his own kin, and in his own house.

I am blessed if *I* endure temptation:
for when *I* am tried, *I* shall receive the crown of life,
which the Lord has promised to them that love Him.

❀

When the enemy shall come in like a flood,
the Spirit of the Lord shall lift up a standard against him.

❀

If *I* faint in the day of adversity, *my* strength is small.

❀

I should gladly glory in *my* infirmities,
that the power of Christ may rest on *me*...
for when *I* am weak, then *I* am strong.

❀

My light affliction, which is but for a moment,
works for *me* a far more exceeding and eternal weight of glory.

❀

Blessed is he that considers the poor:
the Lord will deliver him in time of trouble.
The Lord will strengthen him on the bed of languishing.

Wait on the Lord, be of good courage,
and He will strengthen *your* heart.

God shows *me* great and sore troubles,
but He shall quicken me again, and shall
bring *me* up again from the depths of the earth.

The Lord is righteous in all His ways,
and holy in all His works.

I know that, whatsoever God does, it shall be forever:
nothing can be put to it, nor anything taken from it:
and God does it, that men should fear before Him.

I have set the Lord always before *me*:
because He is at *my* right hand, *I* shall not be moved.

God saves those who put their trust in Him
from those that rise up against them.

He who gathers in a summer is a wise son:
but he that sleeps in harvest is a son that causes shame.

❁

The needy shall not always be forgotten.

❁

God is the helper of the fatherless.

❁

Rest in the Lord, and wait patiently for Him.

❁

God's anger endures but a moment;
in His favor is life: Weeping may endure for a night,
but joy comes in the morning.

❁

I have need of patience, that, after *I* have done the will of God,
I might receive the promise.

❁

The thing which has been, it is that which shall be;
and that which is done is that which shall be done.

The way of transgressors is hard.

God is longsuffering and not willing that any should perish,
but that all should come to repentance.

It is good for *me* that I have been afflicted;
that I might learn God's statutes.

Unless God's law had been *my* delight,
I should have perished in *my* affliction.

It is good that *I* should both hope and quietly wait
for the salvation of the Lord.

Though the Lord cause grief, yet will He have compassion
according to the multitude of His mercies.

God does not afflict willingly nor grieve the children of men.

Despise not the chastening of the Lord,
nor faint when *you* are rebuked of Him:
for whom the Lord loves He chastens,
and scourges every one He receives.

❁

No chastening for the present seems to be joyous, but grievous;
nevertheless afterward it yields the peaceable fruit
of righteousness unto them who are exercised thereby.

❁

When Jesus was reviled, He reviled not again;
when He suffered, He threatened not;
but committed Himself to Him who judges righteously.

❁

Forsake not the assembling of ourselves together,
but exhort one another.

❁

I must keep *my* heart with all diligence;
for out of it come the issues of life.

❁

Murmur not.

The Lord upholds all that fall,
and raises up all those that be bowed down.

✿

If *I* do well, and suffer for it, and take it patiently,
this is acceptable with God.

✿

Be not weary in well doing:
for in due season you shall reap,
if *you* faint not.

✿

Be patient in tribulation.

✿

Bless those who persecute *me*.

✿

Recompense to no man evil for evil.

✿

Avenge not *yourself*,
…vengeance is the Lord's.

They that wait upon the Lord shall renew their strength;
they shall mount up with wings as eagles;
they shall run, and not be weary;
and they shall walk, and not faint.

❁

Fools because of their transgressions,
and because of their iniquities, are afflicted.
Their soul abhors all manner of meat;
and they draw near unto the gates of death.
Then they cry unto the Lord in their trouble,
and He saves them out of their distresses.
He sends His word, and heals them,
and delivers them from their destruction.

❁

The patient in spirit is better
than the proud in spirit.

❁

When *I* suffer according to the will of God,
I should commit the keeping of *my* soul to God
in well doing, as unto a faithful Creator.

Turn not away from him who would borrow of *me*.

❁

Love *your* enemies, bless them that curse *you*,
do good to them that hate *you*.

❁

Pray for them who despitefully use *you*
and persecute *you*.

❁

If *I* forgive men their trespasses,
my heavenly Father will forgive *me*.

❁

Follow after righteousness, godliness,
faith, love, patience, meekness.

❁

Give strong drink unto him that is ready to perish,
and wine unto those that be of heavy hearts.
Let him drink, and forgive his poverty,
and remember his misery no more.

Overcome evil with good.

❀

Judge nothing before the time, until the Lord come,
who both will bring to light the hidden things of darkness,
and will make manifest the counsels of the hearts:
and then shall every man have praise of God.

❀

Men ought always to pray, and not to faint.

❀

God will not suffer *me* to be tempted
above that which *I* am able to bear;
but will with the temptation also make a way
to escape, that *I* may be able to bear it.

❀

Sow a Thought and you reap an Act;
Sow an Act and you reap a Habit;
Sow a Habit and you reap a Character;
Sow a Character and you reap a Destiny.

HOPE

Be ready always to give an answer to every man
that asks *you* a reason of the hope that is in *you*.

❁

If we hope for that we see not,
then do we with patience wait for it.

❁

Take no thought for food or drink or clothes
for *your* heavenly Father knows *you* have need of these things.

❁

Seek first the kingdom of God and His righteousness;
and all these things shall be added to *you*.

❁

We should make known the commandments to our children;
that the generation to come might know them,
even the children which should be born;
who should arise and declare them to their children:
that they might set their hope in God.

❁

Train up a child in the way he should go;
and when he is old, he will not depart from it.

It does not bother me that I do not understand
and cannot explain the holy mysteries.
I do not fully understand my husband, my children and
sometimes myself. I cannot expect to understand God.
I am bidden to worship God and believe in Jesus, my Savior—
not to understand.

❁

Christianity has not failed.
It has not been sufficiently tried.

❁

For by grace we are saved through faith;
and not of ourselves; it is the gift of God.

❁

Am I asking? If so, I shall receive.
Am I seeking? If so, I shall find.
Am I knocking? If so, it shall be opened unto me.

❁

In everything I must let my request be made known unto God.
Of course, He already knows my needs and everything about me,
but He said, "Ask, seek, knock."

Sometimes faith must learn a deeper rest,
and trust God's silence when He does not speak.
There are times when God waits
in order that He may be gracious unto us.

❁

The real victory of faith is to trust God in the dark.

❁

I doubt not the existence of air
just because a strong wind is not always blowing.

❁

I may pray for anything I desire.

❁

I learn to pray as I learn anything else—by regular practice.
My faith needs to be exercised.

❁

Now faith is the substance of things hoped for,
the evidence of things not seen.

❁

Truth is on the march and nothing can stop it!

Open your eyes—the whole world is full of God!

❀

God writes the gospel not in the Bible alone, but on trees,
and flowers, and clouds, and stars, and on loving faces!

❀

Nature is the living visible garment of God.

❀

Live close to the Word of God. This is the fertile soil from which
faith can draw the minerals that make it strong and hardy.

❀

A Bible believer was told that the Red Sea was only six inches deep
at that particular time of year when Pharaoh's army was drowned.
"It was a greater miracle than I thought," he exclaimed. "To think
Pharaoh and his army were drowned in only six inches of water!"

❀

Two shoe salesmen went to Africa to open up a new territory for their
firm. Three days after their arrival one of them wired home base:
"Returning on the next plane. Can't sell shoes here. Everybody goes
barefoot." Nothing was heard from the other salesman for two weeks.
Then came a fat, airmail envelope with this message: Fifty orders
enclosed. Prospects unlimited. Nobody here has shoes.

Whatever I do, wherever I am, my hand is in the hand of God.

❀

God shall supply all my needs according to His riches.

❀

I have only to reflect upon how God has cared for me and my family
in the past to trust His care for me in the future.

❀

I fail not to apply and God never fails to supply.

❀

I believe that God does nothing—permits nothing—
which I would not do myself if I could see as far as He does.

❀

I pay little attention to my interpretation of providences.
I trust God in all instances, whether they seem good or ill,
considering every day a good day although some do seem
better than others. I see my life as one grand providence!

❀

I consider duties as my business and events as God's business.
And I feel God knows His business.

The things which are impossible with men are possible with God.

❁

We cannot see, smell, or touch faith, which is an invisible
means of support. It is the unseen things which are eternal.
If I can see it, it will pass away. However, the things I see
are sufficient for me to believe in the eternal unseen things.

❁

When I am at my wit's end, I find God is there.

❁

He will shield me from suffering or
He will send me unfailing strength with which to bear it.

❁

I shall never outgrow my need for prayer, but I must be careful
how I pray. If I ask for more patience, love and faith, I may need
to be put in the furnace of affliction for God to grant my request.

❁

If I ask God to guide me, He will, provided I completely
trust in Him. He will not deem it necessary to show me just how
He will guide me, but He will give me light for each day.

If I have God, I lack nothing.

❁

I do not ask to see the distant scene—
one step at a time is sufficient for me.

❁

God knows more of all my needs than all my prayers
put together have told Him.

❁

I pray "Thy kingdom come,"
and I work towards that end.

❁

A changeless Christ for a changing world!

❁

May the God of hope fill you with all joy and peace in believing,
that you may abound in hope.

❁

It is good to believe the tangled skein is in the hands of God,
who sees the end from the beginning. He shall unravel all.

I know people in whose eyes I may almost read
the whole plan of salvation.

❁

I am blessed from having heard the Word of God
(and this is how faith comes) from my mother, my father,
my teachers and the clergy.

❁

More heroism has been displayed in the home
than on the most memorable battlefields of history.

❁

Faith in God hallows and confirms the bond between parents
and children. Every act of duty is an act of faith. It is performed
in the assurance that God will take care of the consequences.

❁

Pajama-clad child calls out to family,
"I'm gonna pray. Anybody want anything?"

❁

A little girl on her knees by her bedside told God
the story of Little Red Riding Hood.

A little boy for his prayer said his A B C's.
He said that God could make the right words
out of the letters.

❀

I leave my prayer with God alone,
whose will is wiser than my own.

❀

A faithful man shall abound with blessings.

❀

Jesus became as I am that I may become as He is.

❀

Dear Jesus,
Infinite Wisdom and Infinite Love,
Praying for me to the Father above;
Asking for me what You know is best—
Surely my heart in this knowledge can rest.

❀

We know that all things work together for good
to them that love God, to them who are the called
according to his purpose.

I shall rest content believing that the mind,
heart and soul survive the clay.

❁

And joy of all joys—in my end is my beginning!

❁

The joy of the Lord is my strength.
Wonderful is the strength of cheerfulness
and its power of endurance.

❁

All heaven is on my side.
If God is for me, who can be against me?

❁

What you can do, or dream you can, begin it.
Courage has genius, power and magic in it;
Only engage, and then the mind grows heated.
Begin it and the work will be completed.

❁

Now may the God of hope fill *me* with all joy
and peace in believing, that *I* may abound in hope,
through the power of the Holy Ghost.

Holy Scripture is not the word of men, but it is in truth,
the word of God, which effectually works in those who believe.

❁

God's testimonies are *my* delight and *my* counsellors.

❁

As the rain comes down, and the snow from heaven,
and returns not thither, but waters the earth, and makes it
bring forth and bud, that it may give seed to the sower,
and bread to the eater: so shall God's word be.

❁

Is not My word like as a fire? says the Lord;
and like a hammer that breaks the rock in pieces?

❁

All scripture is given by inspiration of God, and is profitable
for doctrine, for reproof, for correction, for instruction
in righteousness; that the man of God may be perfect,
throughly furnished unto all good works.

❁

The words of the Lord are pure words:
as silver tried in a furnace of earth, purified seven times.

The word of God is not bound.

❁

God's word is true from the beginning:
and every one of His righteous judgments endures for ever.

❁

The Lord will perfect that which concerns *me*:
His mercy endures for ever.

❁

The Lord is the first, and the Lord is the last;
and beside Him there is no God.

❁

God's kingdom is an everlasting kingdom,
and His dominion endures throughout all generations.

❁

Eye has not seen, nor ear heard, neither have entered into the heart
of man, the things which God has prepared for them that love Him.

❁

The Lord God is merciful and gracious, longsuffering, and
abundant in goodness and truth, keeping mercy for thousands,
forgiving iniquity and transgression and sin.

Every good gift and every perfect gift is from above,
and comes down from the Father of lights,
with Whom is no variableness, neither shadow of turning.

❁

They that seek the Lord
shall not want any good thing.

❁

Trust in the Lord, and do good;
so shall *you* dwell in the land, and verily *you* shall be fed.

❁

The Spirit of truth will guide *me* into all truth.

❁

The holy scriptures are able to make *me* wise unto salvation
through faith which is in Jesus Christ.

❁

The Lord is near to them that are of a broken heart;
and saves those who are of a contrite spirit.

❁

…My presence shall go with you, and I will give you rest.

They that mourn shall be comforted.

❁

God will instruct *you* and teach *you* in the way which *you* shall go:
He will guide *you* with His eye.

❁

Cast *your* burden upon the Lord, and He will sustain *you*:
He shall never suffer the righteous to be moved.

❁

God shall supply all *my* need according to His riches
in glory by Jesus Christ.

❁

Because *I* have made the Lord... *my* habitation; there shall no evil
befall *me*, neither shall any plague come near *my* dwellings.

❁

God will not suffer *my* foot to be moved;
He that keeps *me* will not slumber.

❁

Draw near to God, and He will draw near to *you*.

The Lord does go before *you*; He will be with *you*, He will not fail *you*,
neither forsake *you*: fear not, neither be dismayed.

❁

I will lift up *mine* eyes unto the hills, from where comes *my* help.

❁

My help comes from the Lord, who made heaven and earth.

❁

Fear not; for I am with *you*: be not dismayed;
for *I* am *your* God: I will strengthen you; I will help *you*;
I will uphold *you* with the right hand of My righteousness.

❁

If two agree on earth as touching any thing that they shall ask,
it shall be done for them of our Father in heaven.

❁

The Lord is *my* shepherd; *I* shall not want.

❁

Whatsoever *I* shall ask in Jesus' name, that will He do,
that the Father may be glorified in the Son.

I am the good shepherd, and know my sheep, and am known of mine.

❁

He shall feed His flock like a shepherd:
He shall gather the lambs with His arm.

❁

Take heed how *you* hear: for whosoever has,
to him shall be given; and he that has not, from him
shall be taken even that which he seems to have.

❁

… Be strong and of a good courage; be not afraid, be not dismayed:
for the Lord your God is with *you*.

❁

There shall be a resurrection of the dead, both of the just and the unjust.

❁

When Christ, Who is *my* life, shall appear,
then shall *I* also appear with Him in glory.

❁

Dust shall return to the earth as it was;
and the spirit shall return to God Who gave it.

Jesus has gone to prepare a place for *me*.

❁

When Jesus shall be revealed from heaven with His mighty angels,
He, in flaming fire, will take vengeance on them that obey not the gospel
of our Lord Jesus Christ; He will punish with everlasting destruction
from the presence of the Lord, and from the glory of His power.

❁

The Lord Himself shall descend from heaven with a shout,
with the voice of the archangel, and with the trump of God:
and the dead in Christ shall rise first: then we who are alive
and remain shall be caught up together with them in the clouds,
to meet the Lord in the air: and so shall we ever be with the Lord.

❁

Jesus will come again, and receive *me* unto Himself
that where He is, *I* may be also.

❁

If *I* keep Jesus' sayings, *I* shall never see death.

❁

Christ, who is even at the right hand of God,
makes intercession for *me*.

The Lord is Alpha and Omega, the beginning and the ending,
Who is, and was, and is to come; it is He that lives,
and was dead and is alive forevermore.

❁

There is one God, and one mediator between God and men,
the man Jesus Christ; who gave Himself a ransom for all.

❁

Jesus was wounded for *my* transgressions, He was bruised
for *my* iniquities: the chastisement of *my* peace was upon Him;
and with His stripes *I* am healed.

❁

If we walk in the light, as God is in the light,
we have fellowship one with another.

❁

In every thing *I* am enriched by Jesus Christ,
in all utterance, and in all knowledge.

❁

If *I* am faithful unto death, *I* shall receive a crown of life.

Jesus says to us: he that believes in Me
has everlasting life.

❀

If *I* sin, *I* have an advocate with the Father,
Jesus Christ the righteous: and He is the propitiation for *my* sins:
and not for *mine* only, but also for the sins of the whole world.

❀

The world passes away, and the lust thereof:
but he that does the will of God abides for ever.

❀

Believe in the Lord Jesus Christ,
and *you* shall be saved, and *your* house.

❀

Every man that has this hope in Christ purifies himself,
even as Christ is pure.

❀

He that spared not His own Son, but delivered Him up for us all,
how shall He not with Him also freely give us all things?

Whosoever therefore shall confess Me before men,
him will I confess also before My Father which is in heaven.

❀

Behold the Lord's hand is not shortened, that it cannot save;
neither His ear heavy, that it cannot hear.

❀

For unto us a child is born, unto us a son is given:
and the government shall be upon his shoulder:
and his name shall be called Wonderful, Counsellor,
The mighty God, The everlasting Father, The Prince of Peace.

❀

If *I* drink of the water Jesus gives, *I* shall never thirst;
but the water that He gives shall be in *me* a well of water
springing up into everlasting life.

❀

Jesus is able also to save them to the uttermost that come to God
by Him, seeing He ever lives to make intercession for them.

❀

Jesus is the resurrection, and the life: he who believes in Him,
though he were dead, yet shall he live.

Jesus said: My sheep hear my voice;
and I know them, and they follow Me:
and I give unto them eternal life; and they shall never perish,
neither shall any man pluck them out of My hand.

❀

Jesus said: I am the light of the world:
he that follows Me shall not walk in darkness,
but shall have the light of life.

❀

I declare unto you the gospel...
by which also *you* are saved...
how that Christ died for our sins according to the scriptures;
and that He was buried, and that He rose again
the third day according to the scriptures.

❀

He that believes in the Son has everlasting life.

❀

But as many as receive Jesus, to them
He gives power to become the sons of God,
even to them that believe in His name.

Ask, and it shall be given to *you*;
seek, and *you* shall find;
knock, and it shall be opened to *you*.

The Lord is able to keep me from falling,
and to present me faultless before the presence
of His glory with exceeding joy.
To the only wise God our Saviour, be glory and majesty,
dominion and power, both now and ever.

Behold, I stand at the door, and knock:
if any man hear My voice, and open the door,
I will come in to him, and will sup with him,
and he with Me.

The Lord blessed you, and keeps you:
The Lord make His face shine upon you,
and be gracious unto you.
The Lord lift up His countenance upon you,
and give you peace.

Who shall separate *me* from the love of Christ?
shall tribulation, or distress, or persecution,
or famine, or nakedness, or peril or sword?

❁

Whosoever will, let him take of the water of life freely.

❁

Faith comes by hearing, and hearing by the word of God.

❁

Faith is the substance of things hoped for,
the evidence of things not seen.

❁

We trust in the living God, who is the Saviour of all men,
specially of those that believe.

❁

Jesus Christ is the Son of the living God.

❁

Jesus is the way, the truth, and the life:
no man comes unto the Father but by Him.

Jesus Christ came into the world to save sinners.

❀

If *I* believe that Jesus is the Christ, *I* am born of God.

❀

If *I* am born of God, *I* overcome the world;
and the victory that overcomes the world is *my* faith.

❀

Other foundation can no man lay than that is laid, which is Jesus Christ.

❀

We walk by faith, not by sight.

❀

For *I* know whom *I* have believed, and am persuaded that He is able
to keep that which *I* have committed to Him against that day.

❀

The gospel of Christ is the power of God unto salvation
to every one who believes.

❀

God commends His love toward us, in that,
while we were yet sinners, Christ died for us.

The wages of sin is death; but the gift of God is eternal life
through Jesus Christ our Lord.

If *I* confess with *my* mouth the Lord Jesus, and believe in *my* heart
that God has raised Him from the dead, *I* shall be saved.

With the heart man believes unto righteousness;
and with the mouth confession is made unto salvation.

I am a child of God by faith in Jesus Christ.

By grace *I* am saved through faith; and that not of *myself*:
it is a gift of God.

The just shall live by faith.

I shall not be afraid for the terror by night;
nor for the arrow that flies by day;
nor for the pestilence that walks in darkness;
nor for the destruction that wastes at noonday.

I can do all things through Christ Who strengthens *me*.

❁

My adversary, the devil, as a roaring lion walks about,
seeking whom he may devour. Resist him steadfast in the faith.

❁

Trust in the Lord and *you* shall not slide.

❁

For this God is our God for ever and ever:
He will be our guide even unto death.

❁

Some trust in chariots, and some in horses:
but *I* will remember the name of the Lord our God.

❁

Our fathers trusted in God: they trusted and He delivered them.

❁

God's commandment is that *I* should believe
in the name of His Son Jesus Christ and love *my* brother.
If *I* do this, God dwells in *me* and *I* in Him; and
I know that He abides in *me* by the Spirit He has given me.

For as the heavens are higher than the earth,
so are God's ways higher than *my* ways,
and God's thoughts than *my* thoughts.

I am justified by faith without the deeds of the law.

The Spirit also helps *my* infirmities: for *I* know not
what *I* should pray for as *I* ought: but the Spirit Itself
makes intercession for *me* according to the will of God.

Let us hold fast the profession of our faith without wavering;
for He is faithful that promised.

If *I* deny the Son, *I* have not the Father:
if *I* acknowledge the Son, *I* have the Father also.

If *I* confess that Jesus is the Son of God, God dwells in *me*, and *I* in god.

God has made the earth, and created man upon it. His hands
stretched out the heavens, and all their host has He commanded.

I shall seek God, and find Him,
when *I* search for Him with all *my* heart.

❀

Lord, teach *me* to pray.

❀

If *I* abide in Him, and His words abide in *me*,
I shall ask what *I* will and it shall be done unto *me*.

❀

The Lord is near unto all them that call upon Him,
to all that call upon Him in truth.

❀

I ask, and receive not; because *I* ask amiss,
that *I* may consume it upon *my* lusts.

❀

With God all things are possible.

❀

Jesus is able to save them to the uttermost who come unto God
by Him, seeing He ever lives to make intercession for them.

Cast not away *your* confidence,
which has great recompense of reward.

❁

Ask in faith, nothing wavering. For he who wavers
is like a wave of the sea driven with the wind and tossed.

❁

According to *my* faith shall it be unto *me*.

❁

All things whatsoever *I* ask in prayer,
believing, *I* shall receive.

❁

Come boldly unto the throne of grace, and obtain mercy,
and find grace to help in time of need.

❁

The effectual fervent prayer of righteous man avails much.

❁

Ask God for wisdom, for He gives to all men liberally,
and upbraids not; and it shall be given *you*.

Without faith it is impossible to please God:
for he that comes to God must believe that He is, and
that He is a rewarder of them that diligently seek them.

❁

Pray without ceasing.

❁

Fight the good fight of faith, lay hold on eternal life.

❁

Confess *your* faults one to another, and pray one for another,
and *you* shall be healed.

❁

If afflicted, *I* should pray.

❁

If *I* am sick, *I* should call for the elders of the church;
and let them pray over *me*, anointing *me* with oil in the name of the Lord:
and the prayer of faith shall save *me*, and the Lord shall raise *me* up;
and if *I* have committed sins, they shall be forgiven *me*.

❁

God's house shall be called the house of prayer.

It shall come to pass, that before *I* call, God will answer;
and while *I* am yet speaking, He will hear.

❀

Our Father which art in heaven,
Hallowed be Thy Name.
Thy Kingdom come.
Thy will be done in earth, as it is in heaven.
Give us this day our daily bread.
And forgive us our debts, as we forgive our debtors.
And lead us not into temptation, but deliver us from evil.
For Thine is the kingdom, and the power, and the glory, for ever.

❀

Continue in prayer, and watch in the same with thanksgiving.

❀

And this is the confidence that *I* have in Him,
that, if *I* ask any thing according to His will, He hears *me*:
and if *I* know that He hears *me*, whatsoever *I* ask,
I know that *I* have the petitions that *I* desired of Him.

❀

Rejoice in hope; be patient in tribulation;
continue instant in prayer.

All things work together for good to them that love God,
to them who are the called according to His purpose.

❁

Cast *your* bread upon the waters: for *you* shall find it after many days.

❁

Every word of God is pure:
He is a shield to them that put their trust in Him.

❁

Add not to God's words, lest He reprove *you*,
and *you* be found a liar.

❁

If *I*, being evil, know how to give good gifts to *my* children:
how much more shall *my* heavenly Father give *me*
the Holy Spirit if *I* ask Him.

❁

Commit *your* way unto the Lord; and trust also in Him;
and He shall bring it to pass.

❁

Mercy shall encompass him who trusts in the Lord.

The eye of the Lord is upon them that fear Him,
upon them that hope in His mercy; to deliver their soul
from death, and to keep them alive in famine.

❀

None that trust in God shall be desolate.

❀

Be of good courage, and God shall strengthen *your* heart,
all *you* that hope in the Lord.

❀

The name of the Lord is a strong tower:
the righteous runs into it, and is safe.

❀

Trust in the Lord with all *your* heart;
and lean not to *your* own understanding.

❀

In all *your* ways acknowledge God, and he shall direct *your* paths.

❀

Vain is the help of man; God will give *me* help from trouble.

Cast *your* burden upon the Lord,
and He shall sustain *you*.

❀

I will go in the strength of the Lord God!

❀

I will hope continually, and will yet praise God more and more.

❀

In Christ are hid all the treasures of wisdom and knowledge.

❀

By Christ were all things created, that are in heaven,
and that are on earth, visible and invisible, whether they
be thrones, or dominions, or principalities, or powers:
all things were created by Him, and for Him:
and He is before all things, and by Him all things consist.

❀

God was in Christ reconciling the world unto Himself.

❀

God is a Spirit, and they that worship Him
must worship Him in spirit and in truth.

The kingdom of God is within *you*.

God is not the God of the dead, but of the living.

He who believes in the Son has everlasting life;
and he who believes not in the Son shall not see life;
but the wrath of God abides on him.

I cannot be Jesus' disciple unless *I* forsake all—father, mother,
brother, sister, husband and even be willing to give *my* own life.

The Lord shall preserve *my* going out and *my* coming in
from this time forth, and even for evermore.

Through God *I* shall do valiantly:
for He it is that shall tread down *my* enemies.

I sought the Lord and He heard *me*,
and delivered *me* from all my fears.

Blessed be God, Who has not turned away *my* prayer,
nor His mercy from *me*.

❀

God will fulfil the desire of them that fear Him:
He also will hear their cry, and will save them.

❀

He that believes and is baptized shall be saved;
but he that believes not shall be damned.

❀

Believe all things which are written in the law and in the prophets.

❀

Prophecy came not in old time by the will of man:
but holy men of God spoke as they were moved by the Holy Spirit.

❀

Whatsoever things were written aforetime
were written for our learning, that we through patience
and comfort of the scriptures might have hope.

❀

Open *my* eyes that *I* may behold wondrous things out of your law.

Jesus Christ is gone into heaven, and is on the right hand of God;
angels and authorities and powers being made subject to Him.

All power is given to Jesus both in heaven and on earth.

Christ has once suffered for sins, the just for the unjust,
that He might bring us to God...

The fool has said in his heart, there is no God.

Except the Lord build the house, they labor in vain that build it:
except the Lord keep the city, the watchman wakes but in vain.

The gates of hell shall not prevail against the Church.

The earth shall be full of the knowledge of the Lord,
as the waters cover the sea.

In God *I* live, and move, and have *my* being.

Although *I* have not seen Christ, *I* love Him;
although now *I* see Him not, yet *I* believe in Him
and rejoice with joy unspeakable.

Through faith *I* understand that the worlds were framed
by the word of God, so that things which are seen
were not made of things which do appear.

It is hard for those who trust in riches
to enter into the kingdom of God.

He that trusts in his riches shall fall:
but the righteous shall flourish as a branch.

I, according to God's promise look for new heavens
and a new earth, wherein dwells righteousness.

The angels are all ministering spirits sent forth to minister
for them who shall be heirs of salvation.

I must search the scriptures;
for in them *I* think *I* have eternal life.

If *I* have faith as a grain of mustard seed,
nothing shall be impossible to *me*.

Here *I* have no continuing city, but *I* seek one to come.

Commit *your* works unto the Lord,
and *your* thoughts shall be established.

Seek the Lord while He may be found,
call upon Him while He is near.

As the body without the spirit is dead,
so faith without works is dead also.

I must continue in the faith grounded and settled,
and be not moved away from the hope of the gospel.

The end of *my* faith is the salvation of my soul.

❁

Earnestly contend for the faith
which was once delivered to the saints.

❁

This is life eternal,
that *I* might know the only true God,
and Jesus Christ, Whom He sent.

❁

The things which are seen are temporal;
but the things which are not seen are eternal.

❁

If *I* fight a good fight and keep the faith,
there is laid up for *me* a crown of righteousness
which the Lord, the righteous judge,
shall give *me* at that day.

JOY

Every day is a good day—
some are just better than others.

❁

A Morning Prayer—
Father, I thank You for the night,
And for the pleasant morning light,
For rest and food and loving care,
And all that makes the day so fair.

❁

Rejoice and be glad today!

❁

A Morning Song—
Jesus wants me for a sunbeam
To shine for Him each day—
In every way try to please Him,
At home, at school, at play.

❁

It is more fun to give than to get.

❁

God wants us to be happy.

God made today. I shall be happy today.

❀

God is happy when I pray to Him.

❀

All heaven is happy when I am sorry for my sins
and ask God to forgive me.

❀

God has put this joy in my heart.

❀

Do not put off until tomorrow what can be enjoyed today.

❀

The Lord has done great things for us—that's why we are glad.

❀

Joy is everywhere.

❀

If I am always feeling sorry for myself, I should be.

❀

If I am lonely, it is because I am building walls instead of bridges.

We cannot always control what happens around us,
but we can control how we feel about it.

To multiply happiness, divide it.

Not he who has little, but he who wants more is not happy.

To make me happy, do not add to my possessions
but subtract from my desires.

Humdrum is not where I live, it is what I am.

Happiness is not getting what you want but wanting what you get.

I could have things I wish for
if I didn't spend so much time wishing.

Happiness is not where you are going—
it is a manner of traveling.

The secret of being happy is not to do what you like,
but to like what you do.

❀

He who wants little always has enough.

❀

Nobody can take my joy away from me unless I let them.

❀

God gives me all these beautiful things that I may enjoy them.

❀

Life is like licking honey off a thorn.

❀

Joy on account of or Joy in spite of?

❀

When I have thanked the Lord
For every blessing sent
But little time will then remain
For murmur or lament.

❀

We may be sure we are not pleasing God if we are not happy ourselves.

Few pleasures are more lasting than reading a good book.

❁

If I learn to forgive others and live with thanksgiving in my heart and on my lips, happiness will find me—I will not have to look for it.

❁

By reading, I can exchange a dull hour for a happy hour.

❁

I can have more fun at home than any place.

❁

The light that shines the farthest shines the brightest nearest home.

❁

Joy that isn't shared dies young.

❁

Employ life and you will enjoy life.

❁

Happiness is when we feel close to God.

❁

Sorrow, like rain, makes roses and mud.

When I don't get everything I want,
I try to think of the things I don't get that I don't want.

❁

Wealth is not his that has it, but his that enjoys it.

❁

The main business of life is to enjoy it.

❁

I may be rich and have nothing.

❁

I may be poor and have great riches.

❁

Am I an optimist or a pessimist? Do I call traffic signals go-lights?

❁

To be wronged is nothing unless I continue to remember it.

❁

Better to light one candle than to blame the darkness.

❁

I will never injure my eyesight by looking on the bright side of things.

To speak kindly will not hurt my tongue.

There is no cosmetic for beauty like happiness.

Be cheerful, for of all things you wear, the look on your face is the most important.

I am not fully dressed until I put on a smile.

The place to be happy is *here.*

The time to be happy is *now.*

The way to be happy is to help make others happy.

Don't just live and let live, but live and help live.

God loves a cheerful giver.

If you ever find happiness by hunting for it, you will find it as the old woman did her lost glasses, safe on her nose all the time.

❋

Happiness is in our own back yard.

❋

All sunshine makes a desert.

❋

The blue of heaven is larger than the clouds.

❋

Defeat isn't bitter if you don't swallow it.

❋

Each new day is a chance to start all over again.

❋

That load becomes light which is cheerfully borne.

❋

Happiness is increased by others but does not depend on others.

❋

I can be about as happy as I want to be or as sad.

I may be as happy in a cottage as in a mansion.

Pleasant thoughts make pleasant lives.

It takes both rain and sunshine to make a rainbow.

Joy is not in things, it is in us.

Happiness is a thing to be practiced like a violin.

Manners are the happy way of doing things.

The days that make us happy make us wise.

It is not how much we have,
but how much we enjoy that makes happiness.

Laughter is the outward expression of joy.

I consider my day lost if I have not laughed.

❀

Laughter is the music of the heart.

❀

Joy will escape the narrow confines of the heart.

❀

The happiest person is the one who thinks the most interesting thoughts.

❀

We grow happier as we grow older.

❀

Duty before pleasure and neither before God.

❀

The best remedy for unhappiness is to count our blessings.

❀

Do you forget your troubles as easily as you do your blessings?

❀

If I could count my blessings
I would know the biggest number in the world.

Be thankful for your food and drink.

❁

Thank God for your family and friends.

❁

The Lord daily loads me with benefits.

❁

The morning looks happy. The evening is happy, too.

❁

Praise God from Whom all blessings flow!

❁

I won't confer with sorrow 'til tomorrow. Today—joy will have her say.

❁

May I not pass this day in search of some rare and perfect tomorrow.

❁

The cup of life is for him who drinks and not for him that sips.

❁

Acts of love and kindness never die
But in the lives of others multiply.

Rise and shine!

❁

When you feel dog-tired at night,
could it be because you have growled all day?

❁

If you don't enjoy your own company,
why inflict yourself for hours on somebody else?

❁

Isn't life splendid and isn't it great?
Let's start being happy—it's never too late.

❁

For the beauty of the earth,
For the glory of the skies,
For the love which from our birth
Over and around us lies,
For the wonder of each hour
Of the day and of the night,
Hill and vale, and tree and flower,
Sun and moon, and stars of light,
Lord of all, To You we raise
This our hymn of grateful praise.

If I give, it shall be given to me, good measure,
pressed down, and shaken together and running over.

Sow sparingly, reap sparingly—
Sow bountifully, reap bountifully.

Take joy with you when you go for a walk.

Spilled on the earth are all the joys of heaven.

I have feet to take me where I'd go,
I have eyes to see the sunset's glow,
I have ears to hear what I would hear,
O God, forgive me when I whine;
I'm blessed indeed—the world is mine.

Dear Lord, keep us from having our lives so full of good things
that we don't have time for the best.

No joy exceeds the joy of forgiving and being forgiven.

Back of the loaf is the snowy flour,
And back of the flour is the mill:
And back of the mill is the wheat and the shower,
And the sun, and the Father's will.

❀

The busy have no time for tears.

❀

If my mind is unemployed, my mind is unenjoyed.

❀

I know what happiness is for I have good done work.

❀

The biggest reward for a thing well done is to have done it.

❀

Act as if each day were given you for Christmas,
just as eager, just as proud!

❀

Practice an attitude of gratitude.

❀

A merry heart does good like a medicine.

A merry heart makes a cheerful face.

No joy exceeds the joy of forgiveness.

Count your joys instead of your woes.
Count your smiles instead of your tears.
Count your gains instead of your losses.

Discover the great Indoors.

Today is the only asset I have.

Today is the most important day of my life.

Concentrate on the doughnut instead of the hole.

All the flowers of all the tomorrows
are in the seeds of today.

A good name is rather to be chosen than great riches,
and loving favor rather than silver and gold.

Let all those that put their trust in God be happy
for God takes care of them.

Serve the Lord with gladness and sing a happy song.

Every one's work is a self-portrait.

Nobody has more time than I.

Ideas are funny little things. They won't work unless you do.

I will sing to the Lord for He has been good to me.

If I stop to think, I will have reason to thank.

Teach me, my God and King,
In all things Thee to see;
And what I do in anything,
To do it as for Thee.

Be the labor great or small—
Do it well or not at all.

All people smile in the same language.

Unlike most things for which we pray,
A smile we keep when we give it away.

A smile can happen in a flash, but the memory sometimes lasts forever.

A smile is a curve that can set a lot of things straight.

Smile for the joy of others.

The best thing to have up your sleeve
is your funny bone.

❀

There is not enough darkness in the whole wide world
to put out the light of one little candle.

❀

Laugh a little—sing a little
As you go your way!
Work a little—play a little,
Do this every day!

Give a little—take a little,
Never mind a frown—
Make your smile a welcomed thing
All around the town!

Laugh a little—love a little,
Skies are always blue!
Every cloud has silver linings,
But it's up to *you*!

❀

Luck is a very good word if you put a P before it.

Do we enjoy what another needs more?

What word is made shorter by adding a syllable?
Answer: Short.

We cannot have mountains without valleys.

The best are not only the happiest,
but the happiest are usually the best.

If I try to make others happy, I am happier than they are.

Sing with gladness
Banish your sadness!

Blessed is the nation whose God is the Lord.

Those who love God's Name shall be joyful in Him.

Let all those that put their trust in God rejoice:
let them ever shout for joy, because God defends them.

❀

Blessed is everyone that fears the Lord, that walks in His ways.
He shall eat the labor of his hands, happy shall he be,
and it shall be well with him.

❀

Serve the Lord with gladness: come before His presence with singing.

❀

Great is the Lord, and greatly to be praised.

❀

From the rising of the sun unto the going down
of the same the Lord's name is to be praised.

❀

Praise the Lord for His goodness, and for
His wonderful works to the children of men.

❀

Sacrifice the sacrifice of thanksgiving,
and declare God's works with rejoicing.

I was glad when they said unto *me*,
Let us go into the house of the Lord.

❁

Give to the Lord the glory due His name.

❁

One generation shall praise God's works to another,
and shall declare His mighty acts.

❁

Come and hear, all that fear God,
and *I* will declare what He has done for *my* soul.

❁

I was as a sheep going astray;
but am now returned to the Shepherd.

❁

Only fear the Lord, and serve Him in truth
with all your heart: for consider
how great things He has done for you.

❁

Blessed are they that hear the word of God, and keep it.

But thanks to God, who gives us the victory
through our Lord Jesus Christ.

❀

God's word is a lamp to *my* feet, and a light to *my* path.

❀

God's testimonies have *I* taken as heritage for ever:
for they are the rejoicing of *my* heart.

❀

I will sing to the Lord, because He has dealt bountifully with *me*.

❀

God has crowned man with glory and honor.
Man was made to have dominion over the works of God's hand.

❀

God is light.

❀

For God, who commanded the light to shine out of darkness,
has shined in our hearts, to give the light of knowledge
of the glory of God in the face of Jesus Christ.

I will offer sacrifices of joy;
I will sing praises to the Lord.

❁

God's yoke is easy, and His burden is light.

❁

The hope of the righteous shall be gladness:
but the expectation of the wicked shall perish.

❁

The blessing of the Lord, it makes rich, and He adds no sorrow with it.

❁

In God's presence is fullness of joy and pleasures for evermore.

❁

The prayer of the upright is God's delight.

❁

With God is the fountain of life: in His light *I* shall see light.

❁

If *I* ask in Jesus' Name, *I* shall receive,
that *my* joy may be full.

In You, O Lord, do *I* put my trust.

❁

Blessed be the Lord God… only He does wondrous things.

❁

Rejoice in the Lord always.

❁

Rejoice in hope.

❁

Great is *my* Lord, and of great power: His understanding is infinite.

❁

This is the day which the Lord has made; *I* will rejoice and be glad in it.

❁

O give thanks to the Lord; call upon His name:
make known His deeds among the people.

❁

…Stand still, and consider the wondrous works of God.

❁

Worship the Lord in the beauty of holiness.

These things have I spoken to you,
that My joy might remain in you, and that your joy might be full.

❈

O taste and see that the Lord is good:
blessed is the man that trusts in Him.

❈

O Lord, open *my* lips; and *my* mouth shall show forth your praise.

❈

Light is sown for the righteous,
and gladness for the upright in heart.

❈

Who trusts in the Lord, happy is he.

❈

God has put gladness in *my* heart.

❈

What shall *I* give back to the Lord
for all His benefits toward *me*?

❈

God loves a cheerful giver.

In every thing give thanks:
for this is the will of God.

Rejoice evermore.

The Lord has done great things for *me*.

I will greatly rejoice in the Lord, *my* soul shall be joyful in *my* God:
for He has clothed *me* with the garments of salvation.

The Lord is *my* strength and *my* shield;
my heart trusts in Him, and *I* am helped:
therefore *my* heart greatly rejoices;
and with *my* song will *I* praise Him.

Joy shall be in heaven over one sinner that repents, more than
over ninety and nine just persons who need no repentance.

Hope deferred makes the heart sick:
but when the desire comes, it is a tree of life.

Praise Him for His mighty acts:
praise Him according to His excellent greatness.

❁

Incline *your* ear, and come to God: hear, and *your* soul shall live.

❁

Heaviness in the heart of man makes it stoop:
but a good word makes it glad.

❁

They who sow in tears shall reap in joy.

❁

He who goes forth and weeps, bearing precious seed, shall doubtless
come again with rejoicing, bringing his sheaves with him.

❁

God gives more grace.

❁

O magnify the Lord with *me*, and let us exalt His name together.

❁

Great is *my* reward in heaven if *I* am persecuted for righteousness'
sake, and *I* should rejoice and be exceedingly glad.

I have trusted in God's mercy;
my heart shall rejoice in His salvation.

My joy no man takes from *me.*

Serve the Lord with gladness.

Go out with joy, and be led forth with peace.

Every creature of God is good, and nothing to be refused,
if it be received with thanksgiving:
For it is sanctified by the word of God and prayer.

Go *your* way, eat *your* bread with joy,
and drink *your* wine with a merry heart;
for God now accepts *your* works.

Live joyfully with the wife *you* love all the days of *your* life,
for that is *your* portion in this life, and in *your* labor.

It is a good thing to give thanks to the Lord, and to sing
praises to His name, to show forth His lovingkindness
in the morning, and His faithfulness every night.

❂

God makes the outgoings of the morning and evening to rejoice.

❂

O give thanks to the Lord; for He is good:
because His mercy endures for ever.

❂

The Lord is *my* strength and song, and is *my* salvation.

❂

God gives *me* richly all things to enjoy.

❂

There is nothing better for a man, than that he should
eat and drink, and that he should make his soul enjoy
good in his labor...This is from the hand of God.

❂

Let the word of Christ dwell in *you* richly in all wisdom;
teaching and admonishing one another in psalms and hymns and
spiritual songs, singing with grace in *your* hearts to the Lord.

Surely the happiest word in the whole language is "whosoever"!

❀

When the Lord say "whosoever" He included me!

❀

I am so glad that our Father in heaven
Tells of His love in the book He has given.
Wonderful things in the Bible I see—
This is the dearest—Jesus loves me!

❀

The elect are whosoever will. The non-elect are whosoever won't.

❀

Jesus did not say that at the end of the way you shall find Me.
He said, "I am the way!" Happiness is not a station
where you arrive—it is a matter of traveling.

❀

Jesus taught us a wonderful secret:
seek first the kingdom of God and His righteousness, and
all the lesser things which make us happy will be added.

❀

Every day is a good day, though some seem to be better than others.

I shall speak to myself in psalms and hymns
and spiritual songs, singing and making melody
in my heart to the Lord.

❁

I shall bid myself a good day today.

❁

Youth ought to plant all provisions for a long and happy life.

❁

Our Creator endowed us with the right to create
happiness for ourselves and others.

❁

God has given us wit, and flavor, and brightness
and laughter to enliven the days of our pilgrimage.

❁

There are too many joys for me to ever call this life
a valley of tears though there are tears in it.

❁

O the joy of the game of life! Let me keep
a childlike appetite for what is coming next!

To make knowledge valuable,
we must have the cheerfulness of wisdom.

❁

Whatsoever things are true, whatsoever things are honest,
whatsoever things are just, whatsoever things are pure,
whatsoever things are lovely, whatsoever things are of good report;
if there be any virtue, and if there be any praise, think on these things.

❁

Love life and feel the value of it.

❁

There is no way of living joyfully without living justly.

❁

The fear of the Lord is a fruitful garden.

❁

Wisdom will feed him that fears the Lord
with the bread of understanding, and he shall be given the water
of wisdom to drink, and he shall find joy and gladness.

❁

There is nothing better than the fear of the Lord and there is nothing
sweeter than to take heed unto the commandments of the Lord.

The fear of the Lord is wisdom and instruction:
and faith and meekness are His delight.

❋

The Word of God most high is the fountain of wisdom.

❋

If I am trusting in the Lord, I am happy.

❋

I live in pleasure only when I live in God.

❋

God made me for Himself, for His pleasure.
He moves me to delight in praising Him.

❋

If I delight myself in the Lord,
He shall give me the desires of my heart.

❋

The beauty all about us is God's handwriting.

❋

Life, if properly viewed in all aspects, is great.

Jesus said that it is more blessed to give than to receive.

❀

I have great duties and great songs.

❀

A duty well performed is a great joy.

❀

The unrest of this weary world is the unvoiced cry after God.

❀

I can live a beautiful life in my present circumstances.

❀

God gives us richly all things to enjoy.
Knowing this makes and keeps me happy.

❀

Thankfulness and cheerfulness reflect the gracious light
of God's countenance.

❀

Count your blessings. You shall soon be on your knees
praising the Lord for all His goodness to you.

May all your seen pleasures lead to the unseen Fountain
from which they flow.

❁

Every good gift and every perfect gift is from above,
and comes down from the Father of lights.

❁

I can be glad in all conditions and events, knowing God is in control.

❁

That which is born of trust in God rises into rapture.
God gives joy in sorrow. We can sing through our tears.

❁

My inward joy is independent of my circumstances.

❁

No one can take away my joy which God gives me.

❁

One thing at a time and that done well is a very good rule
—as many can tell.

❁

Jesus Christ is the same yesterday, and today, and for ever.

Let us come before His presence with thanksgiving,
and make a joyful noise unto Him with psalms.

❁

By the word of the Lord were the heavens made;
and all the host of them by the breath of His mouth.

❁

The heavens declare the glory of God;
and the firmament shows His handiwork.
Day unto day utters speech, and night unto night shows knowledge.
There is no speech nor language where their voice is not heard.

❁

The Lord reigns; let the earth rejoice.

❁

The joy of the Lord is *my* strength.

❁

Holy, holy, holy, is the Lord of hosts; the whole earth is full of His glory.

❁

Blessed be God, even the Father of our Lord Jesus Christ,
the Father of mercies, and the God of all comfort.

peace

Peace is the happy, natural state of a person.

❀

To carry care to bed is to sleep with a pack on your back.

❀

The peace within becomes the harmony without.

❀

Worry never climbed a hill
Worry never paid a bill
Worry never dried a tear
Worry never calmed a fear
Worry never darned a heel
Worry never cooked a meal
Worry never led a horse to water
Worry never done a thing you'd think it oughta.

❀

Worry—a mental tornado—a dog chasing its own tail.

❀

Anger is a wind which blows out the lamp of the mind.

The fella who worries about what people think of him
wouldn't worry so much if he only knew how little they do.

✿

I do my best and leave the outcome to God.

✿

With God, go even over the sea;
Without Him, not over the threshold.

✿

Jesus prays for me!

✿

The Holy Spirit prays for me!

✿

God sees farther than I do.

✿

Think little of what others think of you.

✿

There is no place to hide a sin,
Without the conscience looking in!

Be sure your sings will find you out.

Fear nothing so much as sin.

There is no peace, says the Lord, unto the wicked.

No pleasure can quiet my conscience.

Money can't buy a clean conscience—
square dealing is the price tag.

Faith is as sure as the sight of the sun.

Faith is as sure as the feel of a loving touch.

Its right to be content with what you have,
but never with what you are.

The light that shows us our sin is the light that heals us.

A clean conscience is a soft pillow.

As long as I stand in my own way, everything seems to be in my way.

When you have finished your day, go to sleep in peace; God is awake!

Cast all your care upon God, for He cares for you.

No one is safe who does not learn to trust God for every thing.

Any trouble that is too small to take to God in prayer
is too small to worry about.

In times when I am afraid, I will trust in God.

God comforts me like my mother comforts me.

Faith is as sure as the sound of thunder.

❀

A tiny seed can fill a field with flowers.

❀

Faith is the victory that overcomes.

❀

Be still, and know that I am God.

❀

When I am still, I know that I am His.

❀

God is only a prayer away.

❀

Take one step toward God and
He will take two steps toward you.

❀

Prayer changes things. Prayer changed me!

❀

God will supply, but we must apply.

Closer to God than breathing—
Nearer than hands or feet.

❁

We cannot go where God is not.

❁

Freely God has promised, boldly I may ask.

❁

To be a seeker is soon to be a finder.

❁

Faith is a gift of God.

❁

We get faith by hearing God's Word.

❁

I cannot have a need Jesus cannot supply.

❁

God sends His angels to keep me from harm.

❁

Faith is as certain as the existence of water.

God's eye is on the sparrow, and I know He watches me.

❀

Though we travel the world over to find the beautiful,
we must carry it with us or we find it not.

❀

One who is afraid of lying is usually afraid of nothing else.

❀

Fear God and all other fears will disappear.

❀

In the great quiet of God my troubles are but the pebbles
on the road. My joys are the everlasting hills.

❀

Faith is as sure as the taste of an apple.

❀

Faith is as sure as the fragrance of a rose.

❀

God gives the very best to those
who leave the choice with Him.

The law of prayer is more powerful and just
as universal as the law of gravity.

❁

How calmly may we trust ourselves to the Hands of Him
Who bears up the world.

❁

God holds everybody in His Hands!

❁

Faith stands leaning on God's Word.

❁

Faith expects nothing from ourselves and everything from God.

❁

Ask, and it shall be given me; seek, and I shall find;
knock, and it shall be opened unto me.

❁

With God all things are possible.

❁

God is able to do much more than we can ask or think.

As the heavens are higher than the earth,
so are God's ways higher than my ways and
God's thoughts are higher than my thoughts.

❀

We pray "God's will be done".

❀

If God be for me, who can be against me?

❀

I know not what the future holds, but I know Who holds the future.

❀

My help comes from the Lord, Who made heaven and earth.

❀

Jesus came to die on a cross of wood
Yet made the hill on which it stood.

❀

God has made the earth, and created man upon it. His Hand
stretched out the heavens, and all their host has He commanded.

❀

Our strength lies in our dependence upon God.

Because I have faith I understand that the worlds
were framed by the Word of God and that things which I see
were not made of things which I see.

God said, "Let there be Light" and there was Light!

In Christ are hid all the treasures of wisdom and knowledge.

I am a child of God by faith in Christ Jesus.

In God I live, and move, and have my being.

I can only deny God with the breath He gives me.

There is an outward me and there is an inward me. Though the outward
me will someday perish, the inward me is renewed day by day.

My body is only my house—it is not the really, really me.
That's why I can be happy no matter what.

Said the robin to the sparrow,
"I should really like to know
Why these anxious human beings
Rush around and worry so."
Said the sparrow to the robin,
"Friend, I think that it must be
That they have no Heavenly Father
Such as care for you and me."

As my day so shall my strength be.

I can do all things through Christ Who strengthens me.

Do not worry about whether the sun will rise;
be prepared to enjoy it.

Take no thought for food or drink or clothes
for your heavenly Father knows you have need of these things.

Seek God first and all these things shall be added unto you.

If I seek the Lord, I shall not want any good thing.

❁

If I trust in the Lord and do good,
I shall have a place to live and I shall be fed.

❁

Trust God in every way every day.

❁

Faith takes God at His word whatever He says.

❁

Continue in prayer and give thanks.

❁

Good prayer says 'please' and 'thank you' at the same time.

❁

God listens to our hearts rather than to our lips.

❁

When you pray, don't say, "hello God"
and hang up the receiver.
Wait for God to answer. Listen.

Pray for others.

❀

A tea party is no fun if there is no one there but me, myself, and I.

❀

Whatever we beg of God, let us also work for it.

❀

Pray our work and work our prayers.

❀

Pray to god for potatoes but remember the hoe.

❀

God is the source of all I need or all I could ever want.

❀

Everything I do is a miracle.

❀

The Lord is my shepherd; I shall not want.

❀

Goodness and mercy shall follow me all the days of life;
and I will dwell in the house of the Lord forever.

Whatever God sends, whether sunshine or rain,
it is needed for that inner me's health.

❀

The ole Devil trembles when he sees me upon my knees.

❀

I love the Lord and all things will work together for good to me.

❀

I walk by faith, not by sight.

❀

All I see teaches me to trust the Creator for all I do not see.

❀

If I can see the Invisible, I can do the impossible.

❀

With God, nothing shall be impossible.

❀

One (and I am one) on God's side is a majority.

❀

To be spiritually minded is life and peace.

No real peace can abide with man who lives contrary
to the Word of God. In all the storms that beat upon the soul,
one who stands on the promises of God has stability and calm.

In the keeping of God's commandments there are
great rewards and peace is only one of them.

Only be still and wait God's leisure
In cheerful hope, with heart content
To take whatever your Father's pleasure,
Knowing it is what Love has sent.

In all your ways acknowledge God, and He shall direct your paths.

With Christ as my Savior, I need neither fear
the present nor be apprehensive of the future.
I am safe and secure in His hands.

God is our refuge and strength, a very present help in trouble.
Therefore will not we fear, though the earth be removed, and
though the mountains be carried into the midst of the sea.

When you can't sleep, do you count sheep?
No, I talk with the Shepherd.

❀

In heavenly love abiding,
No change my heart shall fear,
And safe is such confiding,
For nothing changes here.
The storm may roar without me,
My heart may low be laid;
But God is round about me,
And can I be dismayed?

❀

The secret of contentment is know how to enjoy what you have.

❀

The load of tomorrow added to that of yesterday carried today
makes the strongest falter.

❀

No time is lost waiting upon the Lord.

❀

The prayer of the upright is God's delight.

O bless the Lord, my soul!
His mercies bear in mind!
Forget not all his benefits!
The Lord to you is kind.

Faith is not belief without proof, but trust without reservations.

A grudge is too heavy a load for anyone to bear.

Prayer is so simple. It is like quietly opening a door
and stepping into the very presence of God.

It is not the greatness of my faith that moves mountains,
but my faith in the greatness of God.

You are not a reservoir with a limited amount of resources:
you are a channel attached to unlimited divine resources.

Never think that God's delays are God's denials.

Every good gift and every perfect gift is from above,
and comes down from the Father of lights,
with whom is no variableness, neither shadow of turning.

❀

Do the very best you can and leave the outcome to God.

❀

He does not say, 'at the end of the way you find Me.'
He says, 'I AM the way: I AM the road under your feet,
the road that begins just as low as you happen to be.'

❀

O Lord, may I practice what I preach, and preach what I practice.

❀

Blessed are the peacemakers:
for they shall be called the children of God.

❀

The Lord is my light and my salvation; whom shall I fear?
the Lord is the strength of my life; of whom shall I be afraid?

❀

When the world seems dark and cold to me, I am the reason.

Peace I leave with you, my peace I give unto you.
Let not your heart be troubled, neither let it be afraid.

❁

Be careful for nothing; but in everything by prayer and
supplication with thanksgiving let your requests be
made known to God. And the peace of God shall keep
your hearts and minds through Jesus Christ.

❁

I sought the Lord, and he heard me,
and delivered me from all my fears.

❁

If on a quiet sea toward heaven we calmly sail,
With grateful hearts, O God, to Thee,
We'll own the favoring gale,
But should the surges rise, and rest delay to come,
Blest be the tempest, kind the storm
Which drives us nearer home.

❁

Order contributes to peace in the home.
A place for everything and everything in its place
is a wonderful rule.

We do not keep the outward form of order
if there is deep distress in the mind.

❁

There is no real joy unless we have peace.
The closer we draw to God, the more peaceful we become.

❁

In the keeping of God's commandments are great rewards,
and peace is only one of them.

❁

We are not immune to difficulties,
but we can have peace in difficulties.

❁

How comforting to feel I am in the very niche God ordained for me to fill.

❁

I thank God for His wing of love which stirred my worldly next, and
for the stormy clouds which drove me, trembling to His breast.

❁

I shall not bear tomorrow's load of care.
I shall not weep over yesterday. I shall leave the past
and the present and the future with God.

Drop your still dews of quietness
Till all my strivings cease
Let sense be dumb, let flesh retire,
Speak through the earthquake, wind and fire,
Your still small voice of calm.

And the work of righteousness shall be peace;
and the effect of righteousness
quietness and assurance for ever.

O give Your own sweet rest to me,
That I may speak with soothing power
A word in season, as from You,
To weary ones in needful hour.

No real peace can abide with the person
who lives contrary to the Word of God.

Quiet minds cannot be perplexed or frightened
but go on in fortune or in misfortune at their own private pace,
like the ticking of a clock during a thunderstorm.

Oh that I may trust in the Lord with all my heart
and lean not to my own understanding.

❁

Fear God and all other fears will disappear.

❁

Stilled now be every anxious care,
See God's great goodness everywhere;
Leave all to Him in perfect rest;
He will do all things for the best.

❁

For I the Lord thy God will hold your right hand,
saying to you, Fear not; I will help you.

❁

The more perfect my self-surrender, the more perfect my peace.

❁

Say "yes" to God's will.
Lie quietly under His hand, having no will but His.

❁

Peace is reconciliation with God and conscience.

Peace may be the highest result of power.
In quietness and confidence shall be my strength.

Nothing is worth the loss of my peace.

The Word of God breathes sweet peace,
joy and love into our hearts.

I desire nothing, reject nothing;
all that God wills for me I joyfully accept.
I tell him to pay no attention to me if ever
I pray for anything outside His will,
and I have great peace.

I believe that I have laid aside all self-seeking and all self-will.
How else can I explain this marvellous peace within?

People who are serene and peaceful due to
their walk with God never lose their beauty.

When I take one step away from God,
I am a mile from the gates of peace.

❀

While conscience is my friend, I am at peace.
If I offend this friend, I am no longer at peace
but troubled, fearful and anxious.

❀

Be still, and know that I am God.

❀

I must learn to be contended with what happens,
for what God chooses is better than what I would choose.

❀

It is vain for me to expect, it is impudent for me
to ask God's forgiveness for myself if I refuse
to exercise a forgiving temper toward another.

❀

"For my thoughts are not your thoughts,
neither are your ways my ways," said the Lord.
"For as the heavens are higher than the earth,
so are my ways higher than your ways,
and my thoughts than your thoughts."

Love plus forgiveness equals peace.

❀

If I follow the admonitions of Jesus, I shall not permit my heart
to be troubled. In coming to Him for help, I shall be at rest,
and I shall not fret myself while waiting on the Lord.
I shall follow His leading beside the still waters.

❀

Peace does not dwell in outward things but within ourselves.
We may have peace in disagreeable things
if we yield ourselves to the Prince of Peace.

❀

The world is not in chaos.
An acorn will still produce an oak, not an elm,
and the ducks still fly south at the same time, and
the swallow still arrives on time at Capistrano.

❀

Let us hear the conclusion of the whole matter:
Fear God, and keep His commandments.

❀

Mark the perfect man, and behold the upright:
for the end of that man is peace.

Come to Jesus, all *you* who labor and are heavy laden,
and He will give *you* rest.

❁

God is not the author of confusion, but of peace.

❁

If it be possible… live peaceably with all men.

❁

Godliness with contentment is great gain.

❁

Who puts his trust in the Lord shall be safe.

❁

Length of days, and long life, and peace,
shall be added to whoever keeps God's commandments.

❁

Who harkens unto the Lord shall dwell safely,
and shall be quiet from fear of evil.

❁

Anger rests in the bosom of fools.

The sleep of a laboring man is sweet,
whether he eat little or much.

❀

Great peace have they who love God's law:
and nothing shall offend them.

❀

Cast all *your* care upon God; for He cares for *you*.

❀

The peacemakers shall be called the children of God.

❀

God will keep him in perfect peace, whose mind is stayed on Him:
because he trusts in God.

❀

No man is able to pluck *me* out of *my* Father's hand.

❀

…Live in peace; and the God of love and peace shall be with *you*.

❀

In God *I* have put *my* trust;
I will not fear what flesh can do to *me*.

God sets fast the mountains;
He stills the noise of the seas, the noise of the waves,
and the tumult of the people.

❁

In times when *I* am afraid, *I* will trust in God.

❁

Every city or house divided against itself shall not stand.

❁

Let us therefore follow after the things which make for peace.

❁

The Lord is *my* helper,
and *I* will not fear what man shall do unto *me*.

❁

Be content with such things as *you* have.

❁

How will *I* profit if *I* gain the whole world, and lose *my* own soul?

❁

Fulfil *my* joy, that *you* be likeminded, having the same love,
being of one accord, of one mind.

Where envying and strife is, there is confusion at every evil work.

❀

We should be at peace among ourselves.

❀

Supplications, prayers, intercessions, and giving
of thanks, should be made for all men;
for kings, and for all that are in authority;
that we may lead a quiet and peaceable life
in all godliness and honesty.

❀

They that take the sword shall perish with the sword.

❀

Better is a handful of quietness than both hands full
with travail and vexation of spirit.

❀

It is vain for *me* to rise up early, to sit up late,
to eat the bread of sorrows:
for so the Lord gives His beloved sleep.

❀

Follow peace with all men.

In the multitude of counselors there is safety.

The fear of the wicked shall come upon him:
but the desire of the righteous shall be granted.

As one whom his mother comforts,
so will God comfort *you.*

The wicked are like the troubled sea…
it cannot rest, whose waters cast up mire and dirt.
There is no peace, said *my* God to the wicked.

When *my* ways please the Lord,
He makes even *my* enemies to be at peace with *me.*

The discretion of a man defers his anger;
and it is his glory to pass over a transgression.

The fear of the Lord is a guide to life: and he who has it
shall abide satisfied; he shall not be visited with evil.

It is better to dwell in the wilderness,
than with a contentious and angry woman.

A prudent man forsees the evil, and hides himself:
but the simple pass on and are punished.

We beseech *you* to study to be quiet, and to do *your* own business,
and to work with *your* own hands.

Let the peace of God rule in *my* heart and be thankful.

I may be troubled on every side, yet not distressed;
I may be perplexed, but not in despair; persecuted,
but not forsaken; cast down, but not destroyed.

I shall not fear nor be afraid, for the Lord is *my* light and *my* salvation.

God is *my* refuge and strength, a very present help in trouble.
Therefore, *I* will not fear, though the earth be removed,
and though the mountains be carried into the midst of the sea.

God is my hiding place;
He shall preserve *me* from trouble.

❁

Fret not *thyself* because of evildoers.

❁

God hides *me* under the shadow of His wings.

❁

There is no want to them that fear God.

❁

If *I* desire life, and love many days, that *I* may see good,
I will keep *my* tongue from evil, and *my* lips from speaking guile.
I will depart from evil and do good; seek peace and pursue it.

❁

If we do not find peace in ourselves,
it is vain to seek it elsewhere.

❁

Peace I leave with *you*, My peace I give unto *you*.

About the Author

JO PETTY was the well known author of many inspirational books including *Apples of Gold* and *Wings of Silver.* Her classic books of inspiration have been sought by millions of enthusiastic readers. She died in 2007 at nearly 100 years of age.